INTRODUCING INSECTS

INTRODUCING

Insects

AUTHOR: Pamela M. Hickman

ILLUSTRATOR: Judie Shore

Pembroke Publishers Limited

Pembroke Publishers
538 Hood Road
Markham, Ontario L3R 3K9

Canadian Cataloguing in Publication Data

Hickman, Pamela
  Introducing insects

(Hands on nature)
ISBN 0-921217-92-7

1. Insects – Study and teaching (Elementary).
I. Shore, Judie. II. Federation of Ontario
Naturalists. III. Title. IV. Series

QL468.5.H53 1992   372.3'57   C92-094820-0

Editor: Lou Pamenter
Design: John Zehethofer
Cover Photography: Ajay Photographics
Typesetting: Jay Tee Graphics Ltd.

This book was produced with the generous assistance of the government
of Ontario through the Ministry of Culture and Communications.

For further information on the Federation of Ontario Naturalists and how
you can become a member contact:

FEDERATION OF
Ontario Naturalists

355 Lesmill Road, Don Mills, Ontario M3B 2W8 (416) 444-8419

Printed and bound in Canada
9 8 7 6 5 4 3 2 1

Contents

Introduction

Imagine climbing Mt. Everest every day while carrying a friend, or jumping five city blocks in a single bound or even flapping your arms 15 000 times a minute. Sound impossible? These are just some of the incredible things you could do if you were an insect.

Insects are not only fascinating creatures, but they are also very easy to find and most students are already familiar with a few kinds. Unlike many wildlife studies (insects are wildlife!), you will always be able to get some hands-on experiences with insects and outdoor activities are usually full of wonderful surprises.

Apart from being "really neat", insects are an extremely important part of the natural world, playing vital roles as decomposers, food for other invertebrates as well as many larger vertebrates, and as pollinators of flowers. Insects may be small, but their impact on nature is enormous. In addition to their role in nature, insects contribute a great deal to human society through products such as silk, lacquer, honey and beeswax, and their use for biocontrol of agricultural and other pests, and for medical research.

Introducing Insects looks at the interesting features of insects, at how they get around, at what they need to survive and at what needs them for survival, and how to find them indoors and out.

An introductory backgrounder gives you the information needed for the concept of the chapter. The bulk of the chapter consists of a set of lessons, each based on several activities. Particular background is given to you at the beginning of each lesson. You may choose to do all the activities or pick out those that you feel are most appropriate for your classroom. Whichever choice you make, you will find that the activities provide the focus for the learning experience. In some cases, activities have an accompanying Student Activity Sheet that can be reproduced and given to the students. If the students keep their Activity Sheets together, they will have a comprehensive portfolio of facts about insects.

A large colorful poster is also available that is designed for classroom display. It can be particularly useful as a focus in a learning centre.

Introducing Insects will provide students with some of the basic building blocks of natural history knowledge. However, the activities use a broad, cross-curriculum approach so that you can teach about nature outside of a designated "science period". Students will be asked to observe, to communicate, to use mathematical skills, and to manipulate materials and equipment. In particular, students will be asked to observe a wide variety of insects, and their parts; to investigate similarities and differences; to prepare oral and written presentations; to roleplay; and to draw and construct.

After all, respect for living things and interest in and care for the environment are attitudes that are part of every curriculum. They are attitudes that should permeate everyone's lifestyle. Insects are very important to our ecosystem, and we need to understand their role in it.

Perhaps the most difficult part of teaching about insects is putting away your own biases and possible fears about insects. Emphasize the positive and fascinating side of insects to your students. There is much to be learned by studying insects "up close" but if touching them is too much for you or your students, try using rubber gloves initially. It is important to dispel the myths that every insect bites or that everything that flies is a bee ready to sting. Relax and enjoy the discovery of the insect world with your students.

CHAPTER ONE

Incredible Insects

Take the class on a quick walk around the school yard for a look at insects. In the early fall, spring, or early summer, you should find a variety of insects including flies, bees, ants, beetles, and possibly butterflies. Even in the heart of a city, insects are around.

Being able to identify what the students find is not important; making the students aware that insects are all around is the purpose of the walk. If "labelling" seems to be important to the students, have them think of ways to identify what they find. For example, insects can be identified according to the type of habitat in which they are found, what they are doing (flying, crawling, hopping), or what size or color they are.

LESSON 1

Insect Highlights

Different species have interesting aspects. The following twelve insects can be highlighted.

Cicada
Male cicadas are the loudest of all insects. One can hear their high-pitched buzzing up to 400 m away (about 500 yards), especially on hot summer days. The sound is made by the vibration of a pair of drum-like membranes on the cicada's abdomen.

Mayfly
Life is short for mayflies. Adults often live less than a day — only long enough to mate and lay eggs for the next generation.

Cricket
Crickets rub their two wings together in the same way as a violinist moves the bow over the strings. The chirping music is used to attract mates and to define territories.

Paper Wasp
It is believed that people learned how to make paper by watching these wasps. They chew up stringy bits of rotting wood and dead plant stems, mix in saliva, and then shape the mixture into a nest. When dry, the nest looks like grey or brown papier-mâché.

Backswimmer
Backswimmers can "hold their breath" underwater for 30 minutes! Like a scubadiver, these pond insects carry an air supply underwater to help them breathe. Instead of using a tank though, the backswimmer traps tiny air bubbles on hairs on its body.

Firefly
Imagine having a built-in flashlight! Male fireflies produce flashes of light from their abdomens to attract mates.

Honey Bee
These busy bees must visit 60 to 90 thousand flower tubes to collect enough nectar to make a thimbleful of honey! Even so, a single hive makes up to 1 kg (about two pounds) of honey per day.

Springtail
Insects in winter? You can find springtails (also called snow fleas) jumping around on the snow on sunny days. Look for these tiny black specks on bracket fungus or near the bases of trees.

Common Flea
Fleas are champion jumpers, able to leap 200

times their own body length. That's like an average man jumping five city blocks!

Grasshopper
Grasshoppers can leap tall grass in a single bound. The huge muscles on their back legs help them jump up to 76 cm (about two and a half feet) at a time. That's like one of us jumping a third of the way down a football field!

Mosquito
Did you know that a mosquito can drink her own weight in blood at one sitting? Why do only the females bite? They need your blood to help make their eggs.

Monarch butterfly
Monarchs are one of the few insects that migrate. They fly over 3200 km (about 2000 miles) between Canada and Mexico, making them the long distance champions.

Activity

Focus on insects with the help of a colorful display. Using the Insects poster, set up a bulletin board to feature some interesting highlights about insects' lives. Student Activity Sheets #1 and #2, "Insect Highlights", have drawings that compare an insect achievement to something in the human world. These comparisons help students understand the concept, as well as making the learning process more fun. Cut out the drawings and arrange them around the poster.

After describing the insect achievements, have the students attach a string with thumbtacks or tape from the appropriate drawing to the insect on the poster. The combinations of drawing and insect are: drum — cicada, gravestone — mayfly, violin — cricket, paper — paper wasp, scubadiver — backswimmer, flashlight — firefly, honey jar — honey bee, snow person — springtail, man jumping over city — common flea, pogostick — grasshopper, needle — mosquito, airplane — monarch butterfly.

LESSON 2

Meet An Insect

Over 750 000 different types of insects have been identified around the world. That's twice as many as all the other animals put together. With these kinds of numbers, it's not surprising that almost every student is familiar with a few insects. And despite the variety, there are certain general characteristics that can be identified.

Have students name a variety of insects. Write them down on the board. Ask for general features of the insects listed. Your list should include:

• 6 legs
• 2 antennae
• 3 body parts
  — head (eyes and antennae are attached here)
  — thorax (wings and legs are attached here)
  — abdomen
• hard outer covering called an exoskeleton
• most have one or two pairs of wings (but some are wingless)
• compound eyes — large eyes made up of many tiny lenses fitted together (in most species; springtails are an exception)
• many insects also have simple eyes
• insects are relatively small animals compared to birds or mammals, for instance

These characteristics apply only to adult insects. Immature insects are so different that there are no general features to help recognize them.

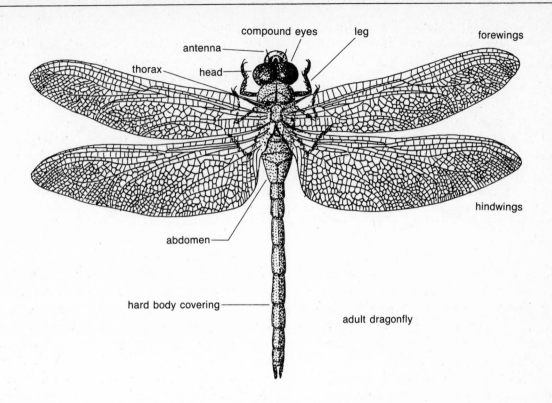

compound eyes   leg   forewings

antenna

thorax   head

abdomen

hindwings

hard body covering

adult dragonfly

Activities

1. Copy Student Activity Sheet #3, "Meet An Insect", for each student. Have students cut out the body parts and paste them onto a piece of construction paper to make a dragonfly. The reconstructed dragonfly can be colored. Ask students to identify and label the body parts or have them point out each body part as you say the name.

2. So many creatures are called insects or "bugs" just because they are small and are creeping or crawling around. But, unless the adult bug has six legs, two antennae, and three body sections, it is not an insect. Insect impostors usually have more than six legs, some have no antennae, and many have numerous body sections.

    Now that students have discussed the general features of insects, have them use their knowledge to distinguish between insects and "look-alikes". After students have completed Student Activity Sheet #4, "Insect or Impostor?", have them explain how they recognized the impostors.

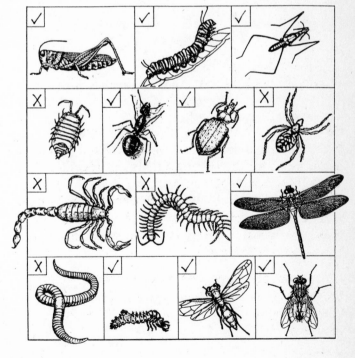

Fact Sheets

At the back of the Student Activity Sheets are ten illustrated insect fact sheets. Each one gives an example of a different order of insects: Odonata (dragonfly), Hymenoptera (ant), Diptera (mosquito), Coleoptera (ladybird beetle), Lepidoptera (Monarch butterfly), Siphonaptera (common flea), Orthoptera (grasshopper), Trichoptera (caddisfly), Hemiptera (water strider), Homoptera (cicada). Each fact sheet has the following headings:

Name

Order

Related Insects

Look at Me: a brief description of the insect

Find Me: habitat

Let's Eat: food and feeding habits

My Life Story: life cycle

I'm Special: adaptations or special features

P.S.: other interesting features

P.S.: other interesting features

Words to Learn: important vocabulary

Activities

1. Whenever projects are assigned, encourage students to use the fact sheets for basic research information.

2. Because the fact sheets have the same headings, students can make comparisons between insect groups on such topics as feeding habits and life cycles.

3. Divide the class into ten working groups and assign each group a fact sheet. Ask the groups to do the following:
   — make a model of their insect from craft materials
   — draw a food chain that includes their insect
   — write a short story about their insect's life
   — design an advertising poster and slogan to inform people about their insect.

4. Have students look up and explain the definitions for each of the words listed under "Words to Learn".

5. The fact sheets (with the exception of those on the common flea and the caddisfly) list several closely related insects. Have students research one of the related insects, and present the information in the same format as the fact sheets. The information, once checked by you, can be added to the collection of fact sheets and used for future research projects.

6. Students can research some of the insect orders not covered by the fact sheets, such as Isoptera (termites), Dermaptera (earwigs), Thysanura (bristletails), Collembola (springtails), Ephemeroptera (mayfly).

CHAPTER TWO

Food for Thought

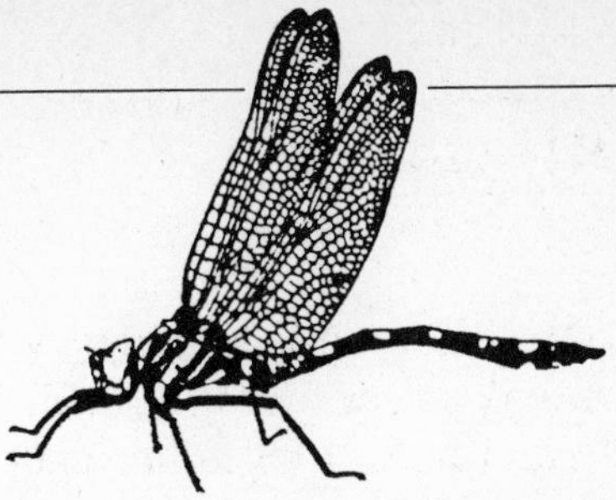

Insects are just about everywhere. They live in air, water, every part of plants, on and in the ground, on other animals and even in peoples' houses. Because they have adapted to such a wide variety of habitats, insects are the most successful group of animals on earth.

In nature, size has little to do with importance. Insects are generally small, but they play an important role in the ecosystems which they inhabit.

Activity

Give the students a copy of Student Activity Sheet #5, "Stream Ecosystem". Look at the various life forms shown. Ask the students what "purpose" the insects are serving in this stream ecosystem.

In the diagram you see insects in a variety of roles:
— food for other insects, birds, mammals, fish, amphibians, reptiles
— predator of mammals (including people), birds, fish, other insects, amphibians
— consumer of plants
— pollinator of flowering plants
— decomposer (the greatest percentage of life energy in an ecosystem flows through the decomposers)

LESSON 4

Food Chains

When one animal eats another animal or plant, a food chain is created. The stream ecosystem diagram shows a number of plants, insects, insect-eaters and other animals that can be grouped into food chains.

Activities

1. Read the poem or sing the song "I Know An Old Lady Who Swallowed A Fly" as an introduction to the concept of food chains. The Dr. Seuss classic, "A Fly Went By" can also be read to the class.

2. Student Activity Sheet #6, "Stream Cutouts" shows some of the creatures from the stream ecosystem. Have students cut them out and arrange them into food chains. They can arrange them in a column so that the first thing eaten is at the bottom and the biggest eater is at the top. You can put the following example of a food chain on the blackboard.

owl
warbler
caterpillar
flower

Ask the students:
— how many different food chains can you make?
— what is the longest food chain you can make?
— since many animals eat more than one thing, food chains often get more complicated; when you combine two or more food chains together, you get a food web; try to make a food web using all your cut outs.

Sample Answer:

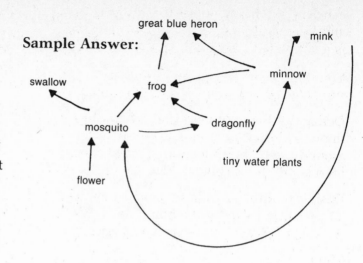

Insect Eaters

Filling up on flies or dining on dung beetles may sound disgusting to you, but there are lots of other animals that spend their lives searching for, and eating, a great variety of insects. Without these insect eaters the world would be overrun with insects. How do they catch their flying, hopping, crawling and swimming meals? Just about any way you can think of. From echolocation by bats to spider webs, different animals are well adapted to eating insects.

Activities

1. You can use Student Activity Sheets #7 and #8, "Feed the Frog" for a variation of the game of pinning the tail on the donkey. Make a copy of the frog's mouth and tape it to the blackboard or wall. Make enough copies of Student Activity Sheet #8 that each student will have two insects. The individual insects are cut out and a piece of tape put on the back. Blindfold the students, one at a time; turn them around once; students try to tape their insects closest to the frog's mouth.

2. Ask students if they've ever been in an empty room, cave or canyon, called out and then heard an echo. Explain that the echo is caused when sound waves from a call hit a solid object, such as a wall, and then are reflected back to the caller's ears. You hear your call once when you call out, and then again when the sound waves are reflected back to you. Bats use echoes to find their prey (nightflying insects). This process is called echolocation. The bat emits a high-pitched squeak. When that sound hits a moth, for example, it is reflected back to the bat's ears. Depending from what direction the echo comes and how quickly it returns, the bat can tell where the insect is and how far away it is. Repeated calls and

echoes tell a bat how fast the insect is flying and in what direction. The following game is a simplified simulation of how bats hunt.

You will need an open space where students can run around, and blindfolds.

Define the limits of your play area so that there is room for the children to move around freely, but not so much space that no one will be caught.

Designate three or four students as Batman and Batgirl. They will be blindfolded. All the other students are nightflying insects.

The bats are placed in the middle of the room and all of the insects are told to scatter. The insects, however, must continually beep in a regular rhythm to simulate the bats' radar and help the bats find their food. After 30 seconds, let the bats enter the game. They must listen for the beeping and try to tag (eat) as many insects as possible. Once an insect is tagged, it is dead and must sit on the edge of the play area. Tagged insects can act as ''cheerleaders'' for the bats, helping them to locate insects. After 5 minutes, determine how many insects were caught by each bat. Have students take turns being bats.

3. Ask your students to each choose one of the following animals and find out what insects it eats, how it catches its prey, and what special adaptations it has to help it find, catch, or eat insects.

little brown bat, spiny anteater, common nighthawk, yellow warbler, hairy woodpecker, bull frog, American toad, garden spider, dragonfly, antlion, striped skunk, chimpanzee, praying mantis

4(a) The ''Attack of the Killer Tomatoes'' is a science fiction thriller about man-eating tomato plants. Comic books and films have often captured a child's imagination with stories of bloodthirsty plants. As bizarre as it sounds, though, flesh eating plants really do exist. They don't eat people, of course, but they do eat insects. In fact, there are about 450 species of insectivorous plants in the world.

Four carnivorous plants grow naturally in our region: pitcher plant, sundew, bladderwort and butterwort.

Using Student Activity Sheet #9, ''Killer Plants'', discuss how these plants operate. In general, insectivorous plants digest insects with enzymes and absorb the insect's nutrients, particularly nitrogen. This extra food allows insect-eating plants to grow in poor soils where other plants might ''starve.''

Divide the class into groups of three or four students. Have each group make up and perform a short skit about insects and insect-eating plants. Or have each group write a story about life as an insect-eating plant or life as an insect trying to avoid insect-eating plants.

4(b) If possible, take the class to a wetland area where insectivorous plants such as sundew or pitcher plants grow.

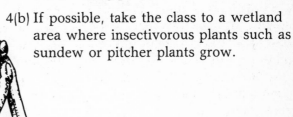

Busy Bees

If you like flowers, fruit, or vegetables, then insects may be some of your best friends. A huge number of native plants, as well as crops such as apples and cucumbers depend on insect pollination in order to reproduce. Without the pollinating activity of a variety of insects, especially bees, there would be far fewer kinds of plants in the world.

Although we owe bees a great deal for all of their hard work, they're not aware of what they are doing. Pollination is just a "side effect" of the insects' search for nectar (the sweet juice deep inside a flower). Many flowers are designed to attract bees by sweet smells, special shapes or colors, or a rich supply of nectar. In fact, biologists have linked the evolution of some flowers to the kinds of pollinators available at certain periods in biological history. As the bee crawls around on the flower to get its treat, the pollen drops on to its body and gets caught on the insect's hairs. When the bee visits the next flower, the pollen is brushed off on the new flower, and cross-pollination (between two different individual flowers) can occur.

Bees not only act as pollen couriers, they also collect pollen in balls on their hind legs, like saddle bags, and take it back to the hive. Pollen and honey are mixed together and are fed to growing bees.

How do bees know where to find the best food? A great deal of research has been done on the ability of honey bees to communicate with each other. When a honey bee finds a good foraging site, it returns to the hive to "tell" the others. First of all, the smell and taste of the food brought back by the messenger tells all the other hive members what type of food will be found. Finding out where to go, is more complicated.

Honey bees "talk" through a series of dances. To attract attention, a bee will begin a dance made up of a series of figure eights. The more food there is to be found, the faster the dance. The direction of the food supply is "told" through a tail-wagging dance inserted into the figure eights. It is understood that a dance straight up the hive wall means that the food lies in the direction of the sun. If, for example, the bee performs its tail-wagging dance at a 45° angle to the left of this, then the food will be found 45° to the left of the position of the sun. Somehow bees have the ability to judge and measure angles from the sun.

Activities

1. To appreciate the complexity of the communication among bees, have pairs of students develop their own wordless and soundless communication dance. The dance must be performed "on the spot", i.e. students cannot move to the actual location they are describing.

2. On a piece of paper, write a location of an imaginary food source. It may be somewhere in the classroom, other part of the school, or school yard. Give the paper to only one of the students in each pair. That student must somehow "tell" the other where the food is, using their special dance. Have a few pairs demonstrate their systems to the class.

3. Use copies of Student Activity Sheet #10, "Busy Bee Maze" to show students how bees collect pollen. If you ask the students to go from Start to Finish in the shortest possible way, they may pollinate about five flowers; if you allow them to retrace their routes, they might pollinate as many as seventeen flowers. As long as they do not cross solid lines, student routes "home" are acceptable, as well as whatever number of flowers they pollinated. Remember that bees can only carry back as much pollen as their hind legs can bear.

CHAPTER THREE

How Insects Survive

Insects are found in just about every habitat imaginable. How can they survive in hot springs and icy pools, caverns and mountains? Part of the reason for this success is that many insects are well adapted to their specific habitat. Some of the basic requirements for survival are eating, breathing and avoiding predators.

The following lessons focus on the different adaptations that help insects do these things successfully.

LESSON 7

Ways of Eating

If the students were invited to dinner at an insect's house, they might be served anything from flower nectar to garbage to other insects.

Because different insects eat different things, their mouths are designed differently.

Activity

Use Student Activity Sheet #11, "The Better To Eat You", to familiarize students with the different adaptations some insects have for catching food.

LESSON 8

Breathing Underwater

How do you breathe when you swim underwater? Most people simply hold their breath and then come back to the surface for fresh air. Others use special equipment such as snorkels or scuba diving tanks to help them stay underwater for longer. What do insects do? Many insects have built-in snorkels and air tanks to help them breathe underwater. Others have special gills for breathing, like fish, and some can even breathe right through their skin, while submerged!

Here is some information on six aquatic insects.

whirligig beetle
Like a scuba diver, the whirligig takes a tank of air underwater with it. It traps a bubble of air under its wing covers, as well as a bubble at the end of its abdomen. The insect breathes the air trapped inside the bubbles, while submerged.

diving beetle
The diving beetle also traps an air bubble under its wing covers. Unlike a scuba diver, however, the beetle's air supply can be replenished while underwater. It can stay submerged up to 36 hours! As the oxygen in

the bubble is used up, the pressure inside the bubble becomes lower than that in the surrounding water. This causes a "suction" which draws oxygen into the bubble from the water.

damselfly nymph
The tail-like structures at the end of the nymph's abdomen are actually gills. Oxygen moves directly from the water, through the thin covering of the gills and into the insects tracheae (system of internal breathing tubes).

mosquito larva and pupa
The mosquito larva, also known as a wriggler, hangs upside down from the water's surface, poking its small tube, or siphon, through the water. This siphon acts as a snorkel, drawing air into the mosquito's respiratory system. The pupa also has a pair of tiny siphons on its head, almost like little antennae.

backswimmer
Backswimmers trap tiny air bubbles on the bristles on their undersides, often creating a silvery sheen on their bodies. They can stay underwater for about 30 minutes using this air supply.

midge larva
Very small larvae, such as midges, can draw oxygen directly from the water through the body wall.

Activity

To enable students to see some of the amazing adaptations of aquatic insects, you can set up a temporary tank or pond of marsh insects. This can be done prior to class or the class can catch the insects on a field trip. Once the tank is set up, give students copies of Student Activity Sheet #12, "Aquatic Insects", and discuss the underwater breathing adaptations of the insects in the tank.

If you take the class on a field trip to collect aquatic insects, you will need

a shallow, light-colored dishpan
kitchen strainers (for a longer reach, tie broom
  handles on)
turkey basters
tweezers or tiny paint brushes
rubber gloves for cold water
field guides to insects, pond life
rubber boots for everyone
aquarium tank
4 L jar with lid (mayonnaise etc.)

— Choose a shallow pond or marsh with a gently sloping bank where children will have easy access to the water. Discuss safety rules with the students before your visit.

— At the site, fill your dishpan with clear pond water. Call this Home Base. Students should bring all their specimens back here.

— Using a strainer, dip into the water to catch swimming insects. Jiggle the strainer gently along plants, stems and under floating leaves and try to catch any insects that fall free.

— Insects can be transferred to the Home Base with tweezers or tiny paint brushes. Some insects, such as giant water bugs can bite, so students should be careful when handling all insects.

— Scoop up some of the bottom muck with a strainer. Bob the strainer up and down in the water to wash away the silt, keeping the rim of the strainer above water. Look for the insects left behind. Transfer these to the Home Base.

— To set up your aquarium, scoop up some bottom muck to place in the bottom of the tank. Add some aquatic plants, securing them in the muck (use stones as weights, if necessary).

— Very slowly, fill the tank 1/2 full with pond water, so as to disturb the plants and muck as little as possible. Do not use tap water unless it is 48 hours old.

— After the water has cleared, add your insects from the Home Base.

— Fill a 4 L jar with clear pond water to take back to the classroom. Pour this into the tank once it is in place in the room.

You may keep your mini pond for several days while you discuss the insects inside and students have a chance to see how they move, breathe and relate to each other. Return the insects to the pond where they came from. This final act should be as important as catching the insects since watching the insects return to their natural habitat is a valuable way of reinforcing respect for other living creatures.

LESSON 9

Camouflage

Ask your students what they'd wear to hide in a forest? a golden corn field? a snow-covered meadow? Discuss the concept of camouflage. Many insects are specially colored for hiding. Ask students what else, besides special coloring, might help an insect hide more easily? The answer is . . . shape. Many insects are shaped like different natural things, such as twigs, needles, flowers, bark, leaves and even bird droppings, in order to avoid predators. Why are these shapes important? Birds won't eat them. A bird will look at a leaf-shaped insect, figure it is inedible, and leave it alone.

In addition to looking like pieces of plants and other inanimate objects, some insects have evolved to mimic other insects. For instance, the Viceroy butterfly is very similar looking to the Monarch butterfly. Why? Monarchs are largely inedible due to the chemicals their bodies absorb from the milkweed plants on which they live. Birds soon learn this about Monarchs and then avoid them. Because they look like Monarchs, Viceroys are also avoided by birds and are, therefore, relatively safe from predators.

Activities

1. Give students copies of Student Activity Sheet #13, "Finders Keepers" and have them locate the eight insects hidden in the drawing.

**Answers for
Student Activity Sheet #13**

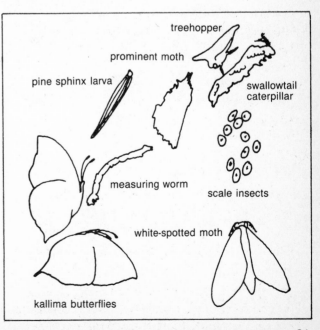

treehopper

prominent moth

pine sphinx larva

swallowtail caterpillar

measuring worm

scale insects

white-spotted moth

kallima butterflies

2. Have your students investigate other forms of mimicry among insects. Examples of insects that mimic bees and wasps include bee flies, flower flies, robber flies, thick headed flies, wasp moths and day flying moths.

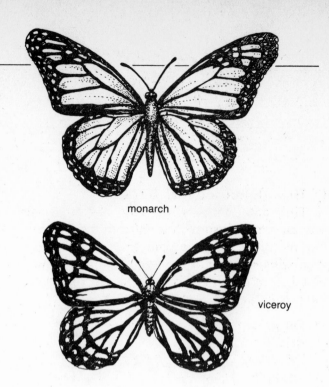

monarch

viceroy

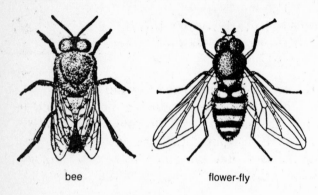

bee

flower-fly

LESSON 10

Self-Defense?

Despite the bad publicity, very few insects will actually bite or sting you. Many only do so as a last resort, in self defense. However, it's the biters and stingers that get most of the attention and cause much of people's fear of insects.

Activity

A brief discussion about biters and stingers with your students may help alleviate unfounded fears, help them understand things from the "insect's point of view" and answer some interesting questions. The following is a series of simple questions and answers about biters and stingers. See if your students can answer some of the questions, before you explain the answers.

Q. What is the difference between biting and stinging?
A. Insects that bite use their mouthparts, while insects that sting use a "stinger" at the end of their abdomen. The stinger is really an insect's modified ovipositor (tube for laying eggs).

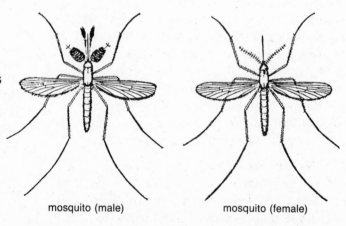

mosquito (male)

mosquito (female)

Q. Is it true that only female mosquitoes bite?
A. Yes. In most species of mosquitoes, the female needs your blood to help produce her eggs. Male mosquitoes have different mouthparts designed to suck up plant juices and nectar.

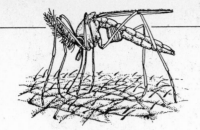

Q. How do mosquitoes bite?
A. They don't actually bite you, like you might bite an apple. Instead, the mosquito's needle-like mouthparts pierce your skin. The female then spits saliva into the wound to stop your blood from clotting. Then she takes a good long drink and flies off.

Q. Do mosquitoes carry diseases to people?
A. Yes. Malaria, yellow fever and encephalitis are examples of diseases carried by some mosquitoes, mainly in tropical areas. Scientists have reported that AIDS cannot be transmitted by mosquitoes.

Q. Why do bee stings swell up?
A. When you're stung, the bee injects poison, or venom, into the wound. It's the poison that causes the swelling and irritation. Some people are highly allergic to bee stings and must get to a doctor immediately.

Q. Does a bee die after it stings you?
A. Only honeybees die after stinging. This is because a honeybee's stinger is edged with tiny barbs that get stuck in your skin. When the honeybee tries to pull the stinger out, the tip of its abdomen, containing the stinger and poison glands, usually rips off and the bee dies. Other bees and wasps have smooth stingers that can go in and out of your skin like a needle, stinging many times.

Q. Why do bees sting?
A. Usually a bee stings in defense of itself or the hive. Only female bees, wasps, and ants sting since only females have ovipositors. In late summer/early fall, yellow jackets become very pesky around garbage cans and picnic

black fly

areas. They are hungry and looking for food. At this time of year stings can be more frequent because of these "bad tempered" insects.

Q. What other insects bite?
A. Black flies, no-see-ums, deer flies and horse flies.

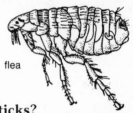

deer fly

Q. Can I get fleas from my pet?
A. Fleas are wingless, hopping insects found in a pet's hair or feathers. Occasionally you may get bitten by your pet's fleas, leaving little red, itchy marks. But you don't taste good to these fleas so they won't hang on to you for long.

flea

Q. What are ticks?
A. Ticks are not insects, but belong to the group of arachnids, along with spiders. They have eight legs and no antennae. Some ticks are capable of spreading diseases to people. Lyme's disease is spread by deer ticks and has recently spread from the eastern U.S. into Ontario. The ticks live on deer and in tall grass and shrubby areas in deer habitat. It is possible, but quite unlikely, to be infected by these ticks in a heavily infested area. Early treatment by antibiotics is effective in curing the flu-like symptoms, however untreated cases can be serious. Lyme's disease is very rare and should not be considered a likely threat when out hiking.

tick

Q. How can I avoid bites and stings?
A. Insect repellant (lotion not spray) for very bad days when biting insects are around. Sit around a fire at night. Mosquitoes usually avoid smoke. Don't go close to active bees' nests.

CHAPTER FOUR

Getting Around

Ask your students how insects get around. Their list should include: flying, walking, jumping, climbing, diving, swimming and even burrowing underground. Despite their size, insects are very "athletic" and can move at amazing speeds and have incredible endurance. For instance, a common flea can jump about 10,000 times per hour without getting tired. How do insects keep going? It's all thanks to their strong muscles and never ending supply of oxygen.

Since muscles need lots of oxygen in order to work, a good, fast supply is very important. Our muscles get oxygen through our blood —

a slow process that can't keep pace with the demands of very active muscles. That's why our muscles get tired if we exercise a lot — they aren't getting enough oxygen. Insects, however, have tiny holes, called spiracles, along their bodies. Oxygen moves directly to their muscles through the spiracles. This is a much faster system than ours — like taking a short cut. So insects can stay active for hours without taking a break.

LESSON 11

Getting Around in the Air

Only insects with wings can fly, of course. But even airborne insects don't all fly the same way. Some insects, like flies, have only two wings, but dragonflies, butterflies and bees have four. What happened to the flies' other wings? Instead of hindwings, they have little rods called halteres on their thorax. These act as stabilizers during flight.

Dragonflies raise their front pair of wings, while lowering their hind wings. Bees and butterflies, however, join the two wings on each side together so they move as one big wing. Then they flap all four wings up and down at the same time.

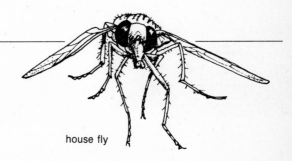

house fly

Like helicopters, many insects can hover in one place by beating their wings rapidly at a certain angle. Hover flies get their name from being able to hover in one place for hours.

House fly	8 km/h (about 5 mph)
Butterfly	19 km/h (about 12 mph)
Wasp	19 km/h (about 12 mph)
Hornet	21 km/h (about 13 mph)
Honey Bee	21 km/h (about 13 mph)
Horse fly	40 km/h (about 25 mph)
Dragonfly	40 km/h (about 25 mph)
Hawkmoth	40 km/h (about 25 mph)

dragonfly

Activity

Students can make bouncing butterflies. Use the patterns given on Student Activity Sheets #14 and #15, "Bouncing Butterflies".

Each student will need:
construction paper
tape
2 pieces of string, 80 cm long (2½')
stapler
crayons
glue
colored tissue paper
copy of butterfly pattern
pencil
3 pieces of pipe cleaners

— Give each student the butterfly pattern to cut out. Each should have two pairs of wings and one body.

— These shapes are then traced on to some construction paper. With a sharp pencil, a hole is punched through each of the dots indicating a "string hole" on the pattern, so that a mark is left on the construction paper below. The shapes on the construction paper are cut out.

— The wing pattern pieces are placed over the cutouts and folded both together along the fold lines indicated on the pattern. Remove the pattern. The wings should now have two folds each where they will attach to the butterfly's body.

— The butterfly's body and wings (both sides) can be decorated with crayons or tissue paper. A butterfly's wings are really covered with thousands of little scales that give the wings color. Little scales can be cut from colored tissue paper and glued on. If different colors are overlapped, new colors are produced. Make sure that the fold lines and the string holes are not covered.

— The wings are stapled to the body as shown.

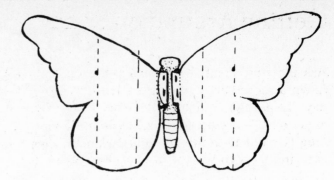

— A piece of pipe cleaner antennae can be glued to the top sides of the head. A pipe cleaner is rolled into a coil and glued to the underside of the head for a mouth.

— Using the sharp end of a pair of scissors, the string holes are punched through.

— Each piece of string is threaded through a wing. The ends can be taped or glued to the underside of the wing.

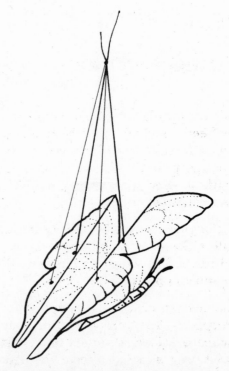

— The two strings are held tautly together over the back of the butterfly. When students jiggle their arms up and down, the butterflies will "fly".

Getting Around on Land

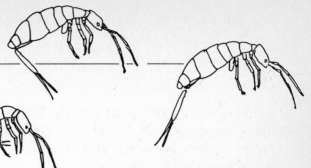

Ask the students if they could climb up and down a mountain, carrying a friend, every day. That's the equivalent of what leaf cutter ants do. A leaf cutter ant is less than 25 cm long (1") but it climbs up very tall trees daily, carrying its own weight in leaves back down.

A springtail has a forked, tail-like structure called a furcula folded under its abdomen. When the furcula is suddenly extended down and back, the springtail shoots forward.

Moving underground is most important to insects like the mole cricket. It has specially designed, strong, flattened front legs that serve as shovels and rakes for burrowing through soil.

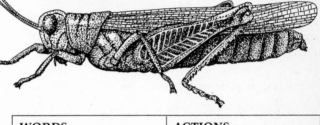

The huge hind legs of the grasshopper help it jump

Walking through tall grass usually sends lots of insects hopping and jumping. Crickets, grasshoppers, springtails, leafhoppers and fleas are all powerful jumpers.

Activities

1. Use Student Activity Sheet #16, "Counting On Jumps", to have students make some predictions and calculations. Answers are 1. flea; 2. grasshopper, field cricket, flea, flea beetle, springtail; 3. the flea is the best jumper relative to body length — it is able to jump up to 200 times its own body length; 4. pogo stick, springboard, diving board, trampoline, etc.

2. Sing or play "Arabella Miller" from *Mainly Mother Goose*, an album by Sharon, Lois, and Bram. The words and suggested actions are shown on the right.

3. Students can make finger puppet caterpillars. They can use them to act out "Arabella Miller" or to act in a short play they have composed. Precut the pattern on Student Activity Sheet #17, "Crawling Caterpillars" using different colors of felt. Scraps of felt, bits of wool and sequins will be needed for "dressing" the caterpillar.

WORDS	ACTIONS
Little Arabella Miller Had a fuzzy caterpillar	Wiggle two fingers on one hand in the palm of the other hand, as if a tickly caterpillar is crawling about.
First it crawled upon her mother	With appropriate facial grimaces make tickly two-finger caterpillar crawl up from palm along inner arm to shoulder. Keep hand on shoulder.
Then upon her baby brother	Take two fingers of the other hand and crawl them up other arm to other shoulder. Now your arms are crossed in front of you.
They said, "Arabella Miller	With arms still crossed, make each two-finger caterpillar crawl up either side of face until they meet and uncross on your forehead.
PUT AWAY YOUR CATERPILLAR!"	Quickly put both hands behind back.
Repeat first verse except last line becomes: "How we love your caterpillar."	All actions as before, except you are now smiling and happy.
	Gently stroke two-finger caterpillar on one hand with fingers of other hand.

Getting Around in the Water

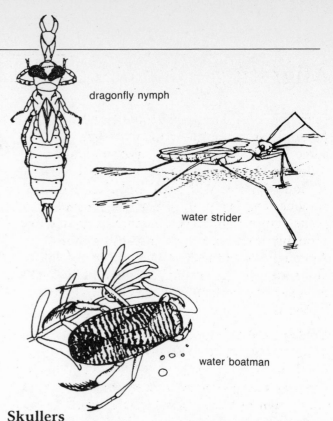

dragonfly nymph

water strider

water boatman

Ask students how people get around in the water. Their answers will likely include swimming, surfing, sailing, rowing and paddling. Insects also travel in different styles, based on their built-in "equipment".

Jet Propulsion

Speed is very important when chasing your dinner, or when being chased by a hungry predator. Many insects rely on their legs and streamlined bodies to help them swim quickly through the water. Some, like the dragonfly nymph have extra help. It can shoot water out of its abdomen with such force that it will take off with a spurt, leaving an enemy far behind — sort of like jet propulsion!

Skaters

Insects living on the water's surface appear to skate effortlessly across a pond. Their long legs spread their mass out over the water and hairy pads on their feet also help keep them afloat. Water striders actually move with the rowing action of their extra long middle legs, while water measurers walk daintily over the surface.

Skullers

Water boatmen and backswimmers each use a very long pair of fringed legs to row themselves through the water. A backswimmer, as you might expect, swims on its back which is keel-shaped, just like the bottom of a boat. Air bubbles trapped on its stomach help keep the backswimmer from sinking.

Activity

Water striders walk on water. They are able to do this because of the way they are built and because of surface tension. Water forms a very strong, elastic-like surface where it meets the air. The water molecules "stick" together and act like an invisible "shield" over the water. As long as this "shield" is not pierced, the water surface can hold up objects heavier than the water itself — like an insect. Water striders have long legs and hairy feet which spread their mass evenly over the water. A water strider's claws are part way up its legs, not on its feet. This keeps the claws from breaking the surface tension.

You can demonstrate the phenomenon of surface tension to the class, using two needles and two clear glasses of water. In one glass, lay a needle very carefully, lengthwise, on top of the water. Make sure you don't prick through the water's surface. Even though the needle is heavier than the water, it will float. Ask students to predict what will happen if you drop a needle into the second glass. Try it. It will sink because the surface tension was broken.

Migrating

Many children know that birds migrate in the fall and spring, but how many realize that some insects also migrate? Insect migration is different from that of birds, however. Although insects will move en masse with seasonal regularity, they generally do not make return flights. The monarch butterfly is probably the best known insect migrator. Although the butterflies fly south in the fall and return in the spring, the same individuals do not make both flights. Instead, it is the young that return.

You can see hundreds or more monarch butterflies along the north shores of the Great Lakes in late August/early September. What are they doing? They're preparing to fly all the way down to Mexico. Many naturalists tag butterflies, just like birds are banded. When you find a tagged monarch, you can tell where it has come from, and how long it has been migrating. Butterflies are tagged on their wings.

Thousands of monarchs roost together at night along their migration route in trees where their offspring return each year. Some of these "butterfly trees" have been discovered in the Sierre Madre mountains of Mexico and are being studied by scientists.

monarch

In the spring, the monarchs leave the tropical areas and head northward. The females lay eggs as they go. The butterflies produced from these eggs are the ones that eventually arrive back in Canada.

Other migrants include the painted lady butterfly, calico moth, death's head sphinx moth, owlet moth and some species of dragonflies and locusts.

Activity

You can make a beautiful butterfly tree for your classroom to celebrate the monarch migration.

You will need:
black construction paper   white chalk
orange tissue paper   string
white glue   tree branch
scissors

— Bring into the classroom a large tree branch that has fallen from a tree. Set it up in an area where you can secure it and where it won't get in the way of classroom traffic. If possible, set it up in front of a window

where light will shine through the butterflies. Have each student make a butterfly using the following instructions. The finished butterflies can be tied with string to the tree branch.

— Fold a sheet of black construction paper in half. Draw the outline of half of a monarch butterfly on one side. Your drawing should include long narrow window-like shapes that will be cut out later (*see* illustration).

— Cut around the outside of your butterfly shape, keeping the paper folded. Do not cut along the fold. You will now have a whole butterfly.

29

— With the butterfly still folded, cut out the window-like shapes inside the wing. You will be cutting through both wings at the same time. To start your cut inside the wing — not at the edge — gently fold the wings in half and start your cuts on the folds. Then flatten the wings out again and continue cutting out the shapes. The black "section dividers" you are left with represent the wing veins.

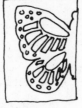

— Unfold the paper so your butterfly is lying flat. Put glue lightly over one side of the butterfly, along the edges, veins, and body.

— Lay a large piece of orange tissue paper over the butterfly and press it down gently. Trim the edges so that the orange doesn't extend beyond the outside edges of the butterfly.

— Turn the butterfly over. The orange tissue paper will be visible between the black veins. The white dots along the outside edges of the wings can be colored on with white chalk.

— Glue antennae cut from black construction paper to the butterfly's head.

CHAPTER FIVE

The Five Senses

Ask students how they would describe a familiar food, such as an apple or banana. Write their answers on the board and have the students organize the answers into similar categories. You should end up with five categories, representing the five senses: touch, sight, sound, taste, and smell.

In this chapter students will discover how an insect's senses differ from their own. With some simple activities they can also take a closer look at their own senses.

LESSON 15

Touch

Insects are extremely sensitive to touch. They don't have fingers, like we do, but they do have millions of tiny hairs all over their bodies — even on their "eyeballs". When moved, these touch-sensitive hairs send signals to the insect's nerves so the insect can respond to the stimulus. Some insects, like locusts, have a super sensitive group of hairs on their head. When the locust is flying, the air currents stimulate these hairs and "tell" the insect to keep flapping. That's why locusts can fly such long distances — as long as they are flying the touch hairs keep telling them not to stop!

Besides hairs, antennae are very important for feeling around. Ants have amazing antennae. Since ants don't see very well, their antennae help them find their way around. Each antennae has an elbow in the middle, so it can bend and move around. Ant antennae feel, smell, pick up vibrations and can even help an ant tell the temperature!

Activity

This activity encourages students to feel different, harmless, substances with different body parts and describe the sensations they experience. The list of adjectives you receive may be used in a language arts lesson.

You'll need to set up and label three stations in the classroom: **fingers**, **face**, and **feet**. Suggested materials for each station follow.

Fingers
Make 4 "feely cans" using rinsed out soup cans with only one end removed and old work socks. Stick masking tape around the open rim of each can to avoid cuts. Cut the foot out of the sock. Slide the leg of the sock over the outside of the can so that it extends beyond

the open end of the can (*see* illustration). Use masking tape to secure the sock in place. Number each can.

Fill each can with one of the following substances: flour, sugar, chalk, plasticine, unpopped popcorn, crushed ice, erasers, cooked macaroni. Students simply wriggle their hands through the sock into the can and feel what's inside, without being able to see it. Tell the students not to bring any of the contents out of the can where it can be seen.

Face

Have a selection of four different materials that students can rub on their faces. Suggestions include wool, satin, leather, fine sandpaper, sponge, towel, paper, corrugated cardboard. Number each sample. Remind students that although they can see the materials, it is only the feel of them that they should be describing.

Feet

In each of four shallow dish pans on the floor, place a layer of one of the following: sand, gravel, flour, cold water, warm water. Number each pan. Have students test the water last, to act as a rinse. Have a towel available for drying their feet. Again, stress that it is the feel that is important, not the identification of the substance.

Divide the class into three groups and give each group copies of Student Activity Sheet #18, "Feel Free".

Assign each group to a station and explain the order of rotation. Allow 10 minutes at each station. Students move to the next station when you give the signal. One student from each group can record all of that group's descriptive words on the blackboard.

Hearing

In general, insects have a wider range of hearing than people. Although they don't have ears, some insects like locusts, grasshoppers, crickets, cicadas, and many moths have tympanum. These work like eardrums, vibrating when hit by sound waves. Other insects have hairs that react to sound wave vibrations. Is hearing important to insects? Some moths can hear the supersonic sound released by bats and can avoid being eaten by avoiding the sound.

Many insects make sound using different parts of their bodies. The high-pitched buzzing you hear from the trees on hot summer days is made by cicadas. They have a pair of drum-like membranes on their abdomens that vibrate, producing the familiar sound. Male cicadas can be heard up to 400 m away (about half a mile), making them the loudest of all insects.

Flies and bees make a humming or whining sound just by flapping their wings. The faster they flap, the higher pitched the sound.

Crickets and katydids rub a raised vein on one wing against a knob on another wing, sort of like a bow being drawn over the strings of a violin. Their familiar chirping is especially common on warm summer evenings. Katydids may rub their wings together up to 50 million times in one summer!

Activity

In Japan, some people keep a cricket in a cage, like a bird, to hear it sing. You can bring a cricket into your classroom and let the children listen to the music and see how it is performed.

Place a male cricket (*see* illustration of male vs. female cricket) in a large jar with holes punched in the lid. Add a small wet sponge

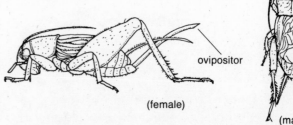

ovipositor

(female)

(male)

for moisture and feed the cricket ground-up dry dog food or chicken mash. Return the cricket to its natural home after a few days.

Taste

You taste with your tongue, but some insects actually taste with their feet! Butterflies, house flies, and honey bees actually walk on their food before deciding whether or not it tastes good enough to eat. Other insects have their taste buds on their mouths or antennae. Some insects are very sensitive to taste. In fact, honey bees can distinguish the same four basic tastes that people can: sweet, sour, salty, and bitter.

Sight

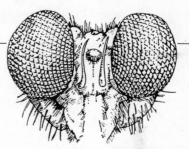

In general, an insect has one pair of compound eyes and various small, simple eyes. A compound eye is made up of a number of six-sided sections called facets. Each facet sees one small part of a whole picture. It's a bit like looking through a colander and seeing through all the little holes. When the images from the little holes are put together, a whole picture is formed. The number of facets in a compound eye depends on the species: some worker ants have only 6-9, while dragonflies have 10,000-30,000. The more facets, the more detailed the image is. Unlike your eyes, however, an insect's eyes can't move or focus. They can probably only see clearly a very short distance ahead.

Many insects can see in color; but some colors are less distinct than others. Usually insects are not sensitive to the red end of the spectrum, but are highly sensitive to the ultraviolet end. It is the opposite in people.

Activity

Bring a colander into the classroom. Students can view objects through the colander to simulate how that object would look to an insect. Students can use Student Activity Sheet #19, "An Insect's Eye View", to draw an object as they see it and as insects see it.

Smell

Unlike most people, many insects have a very keen sense of smell. Without noses, insects rely on smell organs on their antennae or mouthparts in order to help them recognize other individuals, recognize the opposite sex, find food, find an egg laying site, and find their way home.

Ants rely mainly on smell for communication. Have you ever watched an ant parade headed off towards a picnic? Wonder how they know where to go? They're following a scent trail that an earlier ant left between their home and the picnic. If you rub your finger across their path, erasing the scent in one spot, you will see the following ants stop abruptly and then scurry around trying to find the scent again. Eventually they will pick up the trail and head off.

CHAPTER SIX

Multiplying and Dividing

How many students are in your class? It is estimated that there are 200,000 insects for every person on earth. Calculate how many insects your class "represents." Just like people, however, the insect numbers are not evenly spread across the planet. In general, there are more insects in tropical regions than colder climates.

One of the reasons insects are so successful is that they have short life cycles, can reproduce almost immediately after reaching adulthood, and they produce huge numbers of offspring. In fact, one pair of pomace flies could be responsible for producing enough flies to fill the distance between the sun and the earth — in just one year!

This chapter will look at how insects attract mates, the two major life cycles of insects: complete metamorphosis and incomplete metamorphosis, and how some insects disperse.

Before insects can mate, a male and female must find each other. How do they do it? Here are a few of their tricks.

Fireflies use light. Male fireflies produce a flashing light in their abdomen. At dusk they send out signals to the females, calling for a mate. Each species has its own flashing "code" so the females know which firefly would be a good mate (only members of the same species mate).

Some insects serenade the females in order to lure them. Crickets, cicadas, katydids, and grasshoppers use their music to attract mates.

Females also attract mates, often by giving off a distinctive smell — sort of like perfume. The smell tells males that there is a female of his species ready to mate. Male moths are very sensitive to the smell of the opposite sex and there have been reports of male Saturnid moths smelling a female up to 13 km away! (about 21 miles)!

LESSON 20

Metamorphosis

When human mothers give birth, the babies are very small versions of adult humans. However, insect young often have no resemblance at all to their parents. They must go through four stages before they look like an adult. This process is called indirect development or complete metamorphosis. Sound out the word with your class: meta-more-foe-sis. The butterfly and mosquito offer good examples of complete metamorphosis.

Using the butterfly as an example, let's look at the life cycle of an insect undergoing complete metamorphosis. The adult female lays her eggs in late spring or early summer. The eggs hatch into larvae (called caterpillars for butterflies).

The larva spends the next couple of weeks eating massive amounts of food and growing up to 2700 times its original size! It then stops eating and transforms into a pupa (called a chrysalis for butterflies). Inside the closed "curtain" of the chrysalis the caterpillar is no longer visible. It is now turning into the adult butterfly. Pupae on land usually do not feed or move around, however many aquatic pupae are mobile.

After another two weeks or so, the pupal "skin" splits and the newly formed adult climbs out. This adult will usually start looking for a mate almost immediately, lay eggs and start the cycle again. In a temperate

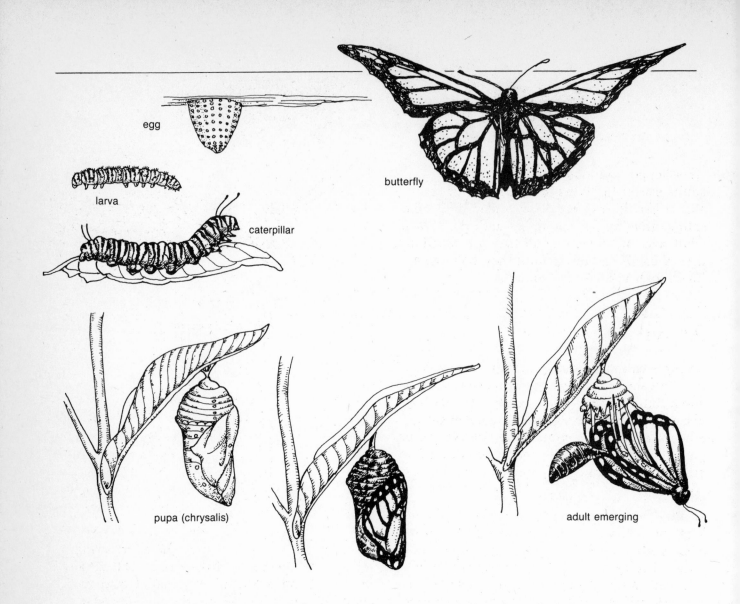

egg

larva

caterpillar

butterfly

pupa (chrysalis)

adult emerging

climate like ours, the second generation will not be completed so quickly. Instead, most butterflies will spend the winter as a pupa (chrysalis) and the adult won't emerge until spring. There may be as many as three generations of adults produced, although two is normal for most butterflies.

Not all insects undergo complete metamorphisis, or four life stages. Some require only three: egg, nymph and adult. This process is called direct development or incomplete metamorphosis. The dragonfly life cycle offers an example of incomplete metamorphosis. This process may be much longer than complete metamorphosis in some species. For example, many dragonflies remain as nymphs for two years before transforming into adults. The dragonfly numph is usually very different looking from its adult form.

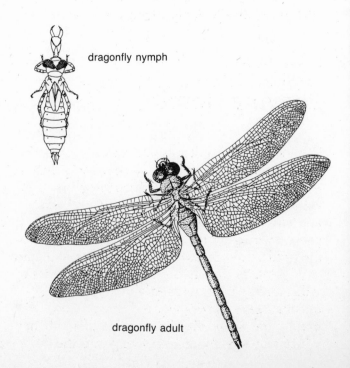

dragonfly nymph

dragonfly adult

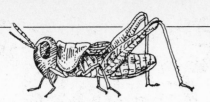
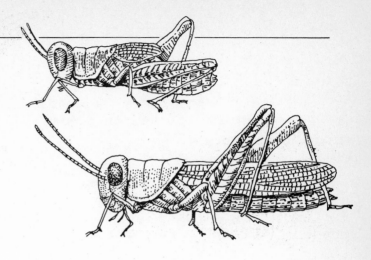

Grasshopper nymphs look like miniature adults except the wings may be shorter or absent (*see* illustration). They spend their time eating, growing, and moulting until they reach adult size. After each moult they are called a first, second, etc. instar until they undergo a final moult and become an adult.

Activity

Students can make a metamorphosis mobile that will show the life cycles of a dragonfly and a butterfly. Have students cut out the insect parts and the sign that are given on Student Activity Sheet #20. The cutouts can be glued onto construction paper, and cut out again. The construction paper side can be colored.

A small hole should be punched in the top of each cut-out. Strings are threaded through the holes and knotted. Use a variety of lengths of string. The disk to which the cutouts will be attached can be made by tracing a plate on a piece of bristleboard. Punch eight holes in the disk through which the strings will be

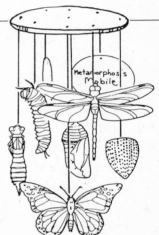

threaded and knotted. If long and short string lengths are alternated, there will be better balance. A thumbtack can be pushed through the center of the disk to secure the mobile to the ceiling.

Leaving Home

With so many "brothers and sisters", an insect's home soon gets crowded. Social insects — those that live together in cooperative colonies like ants, termites, and many bees and wasps — solve the problem of overcrowding by sending specially raised individuals out of the colony to make and start new colonies. In ant colonies, these swarms of winged males and winged females (called queens) leave the colony and mate. After mating the males die. The female bites off her wings and sets about burrowing into the ground to make a new home. She will begin laying thousands of eggs very soon. She must look after her first brood all by herself, but when they mature into workers (sterile females) they will do all the work from then on. The queen's only job becomes egg laying. As more workers are produced, the colony grows and flourishes. Honey bees often divide their oversize colony into two, with about half of the workers leaving with the old queen to find a new hive. The newly hatched queen remains to take over the existing hive.

Activities

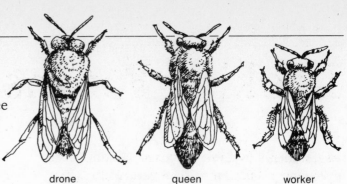

drone   queen   worker

1. Read your students the following story about the life of a queen bee in a honey bee colony. Afterwards, students can draw part of Queen Katie's life or write their own story about an insect's life.

Imagine being born in a little six-sided bedroom with hundreds of nursemaids to feed you day and night. That's how Katie started out life. She was a honey bee. All honey bees start their lives this way, although a few special bees, like Katie, get the "royal treatment." You see, Katie was going to be a queen. At first she didn't realize this. All honey bee babies are fed royal jelly from the young workers for the first three days of their lives. After that, most are switched to a mixture of honey and pollen, called "bee bread". These bees grow up to be workers.

A few bees, however, are fed royal jelly all through their lives — these ones grow up to be queens. When Katie realized she was going to be a queen, she was very happy. Queens are looked after all through their lives by the workers. They get extra large bedrooms while they are growing up and they never have to worry about a place to live — or so Katie thought.

As Katie grew up, she began to wonder what was going to happen to the present queen in the hive. She soon learned that the old queen and thousands of workers had just left to find a new hive. That made more room in Katie's hive and left a vacancy for a new queen.

But what now, thought Katie? I'm not the only new queen that has been raised. Who decides who gets to be queen? To her horror Katie was told that the new queens must fight to the death to see who would become the queen of the hive. She had no choice. Katie fought with all her strength. In the end, an exhausted but victorious Queen Katie emerged.

From now on all Katie did was lay eggs — thousands of them. She was fed and groomed by the devoted workers who constantly surrounded her. No more queens were raised because Katie produced a special anti-queen chemical which was transferred from worker to worker throughout the hive, telling them not to raise queens.

Katie's life was very easy and carefree. She enjoyed all the attention and her very important role as egg producer. The hive flourished and was very successful. But one day something changed. . .

The hive had gotten too big. There were so many workers now that Katie's anti-queen chemical wasn't able to get passed around to everyone. Some workers didn't receive the message, and they started to raise new queens.

When Katie heard about this, at first she was angry and frightened. She didn't want to leave her hive. Where would she go? But then she remembered the old queen. How she had left to start a new hive in a new tree. It would be a great adventure to start her very own hive. Now she could hardly wait.

Katie prepared to leave with thousands of her faithful workers swarming around her, ready to help Katie set up a new hive. And as she left, the battle for a new queen was just beginning.

2. A board game that gives students a peek at what a mosquito's life might be like is given on Student Activity Sheet #21, "Meet A Mosquito". Make several copies of the game and glue onto cardboard. If you can laminate them, they'll last longer. Two to four students can play. You will need different colored buttons, one for each player, and one die for each game. Review the instructions.

CHAPTER SEVEN

Looking For Insects

Ask students to name an insect. Chances are everyone is familiar with several insects, whether they like them or not. Insects are everywhere outside in all seasons, and, sometimes insects are in our homes. Insects are great hitchhikers, coming in on shoes, clothes, pets, food, and flowers.

LESSON 22

In The Winter

You may think of insects only during the spring and summer when they're buzzing and crawling around, but insect watching can be a year-round activity. Take your class on a winter insect hike, and see what evidence of insects you can find. Whether they're active or hibernating, finding insects in winter can be lots of fun.

Remember to go over standard safety rules with the class before your hike. Never let children walk on untested ice and avoid steep banks.

Activities

1. Insects in winter? Surprisingly enough, there are several species that stay active in the winter or that come out during thaws. You can find snow fleas on the snow, water boatmen, backswimmers, diving beetles and sometimes water striders around the ice on ponds, especially on warmer days, and stoneflies can be spotted near fast-flowing, ice-free streams. You may even spot a mourning cloak butterfly or honey bee flitting around on a mild day.

    Before your hike, hand out the winter scene illustration on Student Activity Sheet #22, "Winter Insect Hike". Identify the active insects with your students.

    Besides the active insects, you can also look for hibernating insects. They may be hard to recognize, since insects hibernate in different stages — as eggs, larvae,

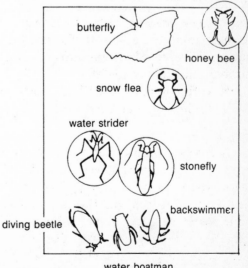

Answers for Student Activity Sheet #22

butterfly

honey bee

snow flea

water strider

stonefly

backswimmer

diving beetle

water boatman

nymphs, pupae, or adults. You can share with the students Student Activity Sheet #23, "Mini-Guide to Hibernating Insects".

2.(a) You can look for goldenrod plants with a gall on the stems during the insect hike or you can bring a sample into the classroom. Ask students what they think caused the "bump" or gall in the stem. It happens when a fly or moth moves into the stem for the winter.

An adult fly (round gall) or moth (egg-shaped gall) lays an egg on the plant's stem. When the egg hatches, the larva — a little, white grub — crawls along the stem, chews a hole, and then crawls inside the stem. The plant responds to this invasion by growing extra, thick layers of plant tissue around the grub. This extra tissue forms the gall.

Inside the gall, the growing larva is in insect heaven. It's surrounded by food — the plant itself, it is hidden from predators such as chickadees and downy woodpeckers, and it is safe from the winter's cold.

Most gall insects spend winter as larvae and then change into pupae in early spring. By late spring or early summer, they've turned into adults. How do they get out? Before pupating, the larva chews a little exit hole for the adult to come out, completing the life cycle.

You can collect galls in the field and take a closer look at them. You can also raise the larvae in your classroom to see what kind of gall insect will emerge.

What to do:
In winter (or late summer/early fall), take a walk through a patch of goldenrod and collect several galls. Try to collect round and egg-shaped galls. Use scissors to cut the stems.

goldenrod gall

With the pen knife, carefully cut a gall open to see what's inside. Before looking, ask the students to predict what the grub will look like — size, color, shape. If the gall is empty, look for any escape holes. Ask students what they think may have happened to the grub. Here are some suggestions. The adult may have emerged earlier in the year, or a hungry bird may have discovered the hidden larva. Sometimes you'll find an unexpected guest. It may be a parasite that has killed the gall maker, or it may be a spider or ant that has moved into an empty gall.

Place the rest of your unopened galls into a bag and take them back to the classroom.

Put a few samples of each shape of gall in jars covered with screening, secured with elastics.

Put the jars in an unheated area and leave them for several months.

In late spring, bring the jars back inside. Watch for the emergence of the tiny adult insects.

2.(b) In the past, people boiled galls to extract their pigments. You can try boiling some of your galls to see what color of natural dye you can get.

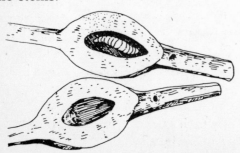

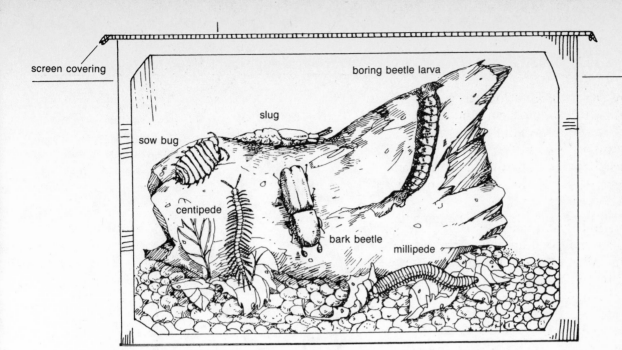

screen covering

boring beetle larva

slug

sow bug

centipede

bark beetle

millipede

3. Before the weather's cold and snowy, you can bring a piece of nature indoors and watch some woodland insects all winter long. All you need is a terrarium, such as a glass jar or aquarium with a screen cover and . . .

pebbles or sand
small, untreated charcoal pieces
soil from the woods, including leaf litter
part of a rotting log
some woodland plants and mosses from
    around the log
water
plant mister
a trowel

What to do:
Place a layer of small pebbles or sand on the bottom of your terrarium for drainage. Sprinkle a thin layer of charcoal pieces over the sand to keep the soil fresh.

Take your terrarium to the woods in the early fall and find a small rotting log, full of life. Remember, you can't dig in parks, conservation areas, or nature reserves. If you're on private land, be sure to get permission first.

Add the soil and leaf litter so that it is 5-7 cm (about two inches) thick. Moisten the earth slightly and shape it into small hills.

Carefully break off a piece of the rotting log including bark, wood, and some soil from below. Take as large a piece as will fit in the terrarium, but don't squish it in. Take only a few specimens to disturb the area as little as possible.

Dig up some of the mosses and small plants growing around the log. Plant them in your terrarium. Press the plants down firmly and dampen with water. Your terrarium should be kept moist with the mister, but not soaked.

Place the screen over the tank and secure it with tape.

In the classroom, place your container in an area where it will get some natural sunlight, fresh air, and temperatures between 18-24°C (about 70°F). Avoid excessive direct sunlight, dry heat, or drafts. When you're finished with your terrarium, be sure to return the creatures to their original homes when the weather is warm again.

Have your students take notes about what they see in the terrarium. Assign one or two students to watch the terrarium for a different, specified time period every day. They should try to make a list or sketch of all the creatures they see. Have them answer these questions:
— what is the color, size, shape, number of legs, etc. of each animal?
— which ones are insects and which are non-insects?

— where do the different creatures live?
— do they move around or stay in one place?
— how do they move?
— are they more active at different times of day?
— what do they eat?
— what do the animals use the plants and soil for?

LESSON 23

In The Fields

Just about every plant you can think of is food or shelter to one or more kinds of insects. Insects can be found on roots, stems, leaves, flowers, seeds, bark, and even inside plants. In late spring and early summer your class can go on an insect adventure in a field of tall grass or other unmown place. With some simple equipment, you'll find dozens of different-looking insects.

Emphasize with the students that knowing the names of all the insects found is not important. Teachers don't need to know them either! Try to identify insects in different ways — by color, size, or shape. The silhouettes of insects found on Student Activity Sheet #26

4. Use Student Activity Sheet #24, "Insects In Code" to familiarize students with the names of insects they might find on a winter insect hike. Answers: 1. snow flea; 2. stonefly; 3. water boatman; 4. mourning cloak butterfly; 5. bagworm eggs; 6. moth cocoon

might be helpful for the shapes. The variety and availability of insect life lends itself to successful outdoor activities for all ages.

Activities

1. This activity is geared for primary students. Copy and hand out Student Activity Sheet #25, "Flower Feeders" to each student. Have them cut out the whole plant and glue it to a piece of construction paper. Ask students to cut out each flower feeding insect and glue it to the correct part of the plant. Discuss what part each insect feeds on before students begin:

    aphid: crawls on the stem and sucks juices out of the stem
    ladybug: crawls on the stem and feeds on aphids

    bumble bee: sits right in the flower and sucks nectar
    caterpillar: crawls on leaves, eating the leaves

    After the insects are in place, students can color their picture.

2. Use Student Activity Sheet #26, "Feasting On Flowers" to help students identify insects they might find on a hike. Warn them that there are twenty flower feeders plus four insect eaters. Can they identify the insect eaters?

Feasting On Flowers

Circle the insects; put a colored circle around the insect eaters.

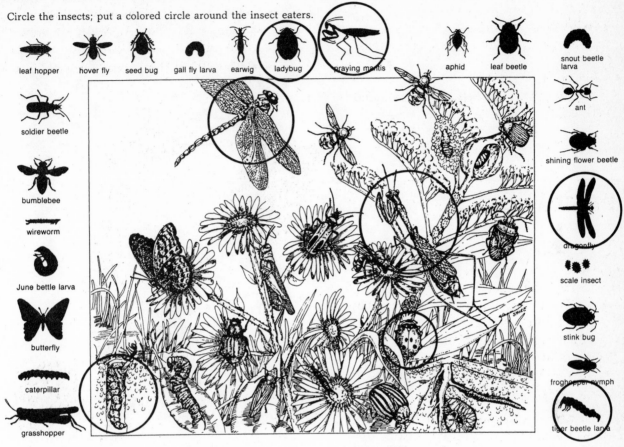

leaf hopper · hover fly · seed bug · gall fly larva · earwig · ladybug · praying mantis · aphid · leaf beetle · snout beetle larva

soldier beetle

bumblebee

wireworm

June beetle larva

butterfly

caterpillar

grasshopper

ant

shining flower beetle

dragonfly

scale insect

stink bug

froghopper nymph

tiger beetle larva

The four insect eaters are: ladybug, praying mantis, tiger beetle larva, dragonfly

3.(a) You can use Student Activity Sheet #26 as a mini-guide for this activity.

Take the class out in late May or June to an unmown field, ditch, or similar place. The main objective of this activity is for students to discover the variety and abundance of insect life. Many have seen insects hopping or flying away when they walk through tall grass, but few students get a chance to really look at the insects living there. This activity also gives you a chance to develop within children a respect for insects and perhaps to alleviate unfounded fears. If you don't mind insects crawling on your hands and arms, this demonstration may help your students relax in the presence of "bugs".

You will need:
sweep nets
bug boxes or clear pill bottles with lids with holes punched in
large clear jam jars with lids with holes punched in
tweezers

What to do:
Have students simply walk through the grass or sit quietly in a patch of tall grass for five or so minutes, just to observe the natural activity of insects in this habitat before trying to collect anything for a closer look. Ask students to listen as well as watch for insects.

Drag sweep nets through the tall grass and wildflowers.

When you catch something, carefully transfer it with tweezers, or your fingers, to a pill bottle or bug box. If the insect is very large — like a praying mantis or large grasshopper — place it in a large jam jar.

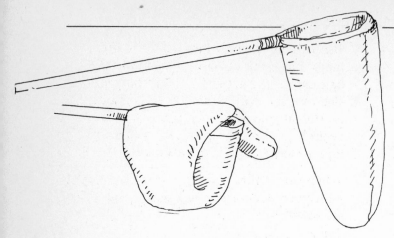

To keep insects in your net from escaping while you are getting a closer look at something, fold the hanging part of your net up over the open end (*see* illustration).

When you've finished looking at the insects, carefully return them to where they were found. Do not leave captive insects in the sun, particularly those in bug boxes.

For each insect, ask students to point out its features and describe its overall shape and color.

3.(b) On your "sweeping" hike, you might find evidence of "spittle bugs". The sudsy masses on grasses and weeds reveal some surprising secrets. The white foam is produced from plant juices by the nymphs of froghoppers, little frog-like insects that hop from plant to plant. A nymph is the life stage before the froghopper becomes an adult. The "spit" hides the nymph from predators and keeps it moist. When you find a mass of "spit", gently move some of the foam away with your finger to find the nymph inside. Be sure to move the foam back over the insect before you go.

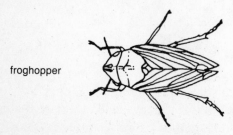

froghopper

4. Give students copies of Student Activity Sheet #27, "Insect Artists". Ask them to match the insect with its "art" by reading the clues, and to name each insect. Answers are: 1. carpenter ant; 2. engraver beetle; 3. gall fly; 4. leaf miner beetle larva

5. When you're on an insect hunt with your students, have them try a few of these tricks to tempt well-hidden insects out from their shelters. For all of the activities, take along some standard insect hunting "tools": magnifying glasses or bug boxes, tweezers, and clear pill bottles so insects can be seen close up temporarily. Before collecting, have students observe any insects in their natural habitat first.

Trick #1: Shaking
You will need an old white sheet to spread under a bush or low tree. Shake the branches. As well as loose plant material, several different kinds of insects should fall onto the sheet. Have a closer look at the insects, and then return them gently to a spot under the shrub. They will crawl or fly back to their home.

If you shake several bushes, did you find different insects from different bushes? Did some have a greater number of insects?

Trick #2: Baiting
Make up a mixture of fruit juice (stale beer works even better), mashed, ripe fruit such as bananas, and sugar or molasses. With an old paint brush, paint the mixture onto the base of tree trunks, fallen logs, etc. Dig a small hole, big enough for a rinsed out soup can; drop some of the mixture in the can and around the rim, and put the can in the hole. Leave the baited area for about twenty minutes. On your return, what insects have been attracted to the bait? Which location attracted the most insects? Be sure to remove the can and fill in the hole before you leave.

Trick #3: Decomposition

The role of insects in decomposition is often overlooked. In a mature forest, 90% of the ecosystem's energy passes through the decomposers' community, or detrivore cycle, while only 10% goes through the "normal" food chain. In addition, the mostly unknown decomposers, such as dung beetles and flies, are very important in controlling bacterial blooms that would run rampant in the spring or during heavy rains.

This activity suggestion, although smelly, can help students discover some of the unseen decomposers that abound. It is recommended that only the teacher handle the chicken.

You will need:
a piece of chicken (uncooked)
rubber gloves
a jar with a lid
rinsed out soup can
large gauge wire mesh to fit over can
tape
tweezers

What to do:
Leave the chicken to rot in the jar out of the refrigerator for a few days.

Use rubber gloves when handling the meat. Place the chicken outside in your bait can in the ground for an hour or so. The chicken will be smelly so it is best to do this at some distance from buildings. Secure the wire mesh over the can with tape to keep larger animals away.

When you return, pick the chicken apart with your tweezers to see what you attracted.

Trick #4: Peeking

When hiking, have students carefully overturn stones, rocks, and small rotting logs. Many insects and other animals shelter under these terrific hiding places and often go unnoticed. Be sure that students replace all overturned items carefully to their original positions so that the animals remain protected. What might you find? Here is a partial list: insects such as various beetles, ants, earwigs and crickets, as well as non-insects like wood lice, centipedes, millipedes, slugs, snails, earthworms, and maybe even a newt or salamander.

LESSON 24

In Our Homes

This lesson will look at homebody insects, as well as other ways insects affect us all — in art, music, and literature.

Activities

1. Ask your students to do an insect hunt at home. The best places to look are around fresh fruit (fruit flies), in old cereal, stored grain or flour in kitchen cupboards (weevils, flour beetles, maggots), basements (crickets, earwigs), near doors (ants), on window sills (house flies, ladybugs, wasps or bees), in storage closets or attics (clothes moths) or on house plants (aphids, mealy bugs, whiteflies). Be sure to emphasize that all

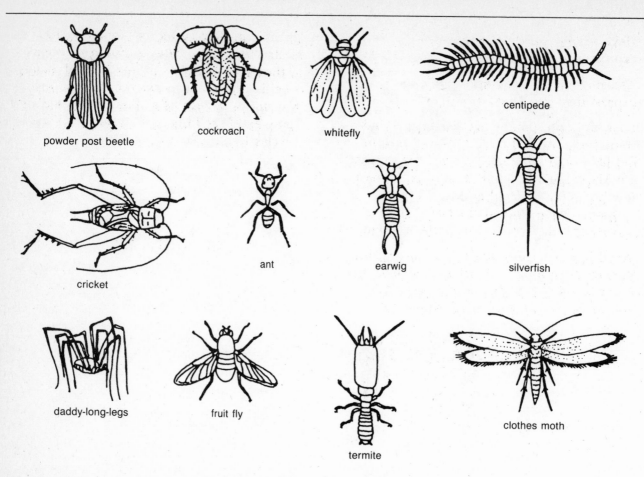

powder post beetle

cockroach

whitefly

centipede

cricket

ant

earwig

silverfish

daddy-long-legs

fruit fly

termite

clothes moth

houses have a few insects from time to time and that it is not an indication of poor housekeeping!

Students can bring their insects into class in jars with holes punched in the lids. Discuss the different insects they have found.

Make a display of household insects on your bulletin board by putting up a large shell of a house, divided into attic, main floor and basement. Have students draw and cut out pictures of some of the insects found and glue them in place on your display. Other insects may be added.

2. Distribute Student Activity Sheet #28, "Hunting For Insects At Home". This is a word search. The words may be found up or down, frontwards or backwards, and diagonally.

Answers:

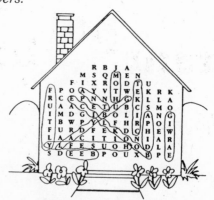

3. Several common expressions involve the names of insects. Ask students to find out the meaning of the following expressions:

"a bee in your bonnet"
"breeding like flies"
"don't bug me"
"to be a fly on the wall"
"ants in your pants"
"a busy bee"
"a hive of activity"
"a fly in the ointment"

46

Have students try using each of the expressions in sentences or a short story.

Ask students to think up some new expressions, using insects.

4. Look through some music books and find some insect-related songs. "There was an old lady who swallowed a fly", "The Ants Go Marching . . .", and "Inchworm" are a few possibilities. Hold an insect theme singsong. Have students make up actions to accompany the words, and perform them.

5. Word pictures try to create an image using the combination of a word and the way the word is presented. The design should appear as part of the letters. Examples:

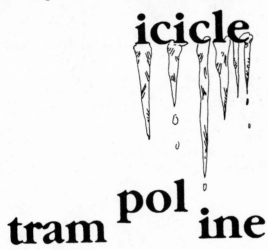

Have students think up and draw their own insect-related word pictures.

6. Check your library for children's books related to insects. Offer a display of books in the classroom for children to read during specified times, or to borrow. Choose one or two stories to read as a class. There are also many excellent films and videos available for classroom use.

CHAPTER EIGHT

Insects In Jeopardy

Karner Blue

A species listed as endangered is believed to be threatened with immediate disappearance throughout all or a significant portion of its range. When a species becomes extinct, there are no individuals alive anywhere in the world — they are gone forever. For example, Ontario has only two insect species designated as endangered: the Karner Blue Butterfly and the Frosted Elfin. The West Virginia White Butterfly which was previously listed as endangered was taken off the list since it was believed to be no longer endangered.

Explain to students that if they lost their home, had no food, and nowhere to go for protection, their lives would be in danger. This is what is facing endangered species all over the world. Their habitat is being destroyed and they have nowhere else to live, feed, breed, or hide from enemies. Habitat loss is the biggest problem facing endangered species.

Since Monarch butterflies migrate to Mexico each winter, they rely on their Mexican habitat too. Over the past few years, the forest where they live in Mexico has been disappearing due to logging and clearing for farming. This loss of habitat may be a serious threat to Monarchs if it continues.

The Karner Blue and Frosted Elfin butterflies have suffered from loss of habitat due to natural succession at one of their known habitats in the Forest Nursery Headquarters near St. Williams, Ontario. These butterflies rely totally on a plant called wild lupine which requires open areas in which to grow. Heavy planting of trees as well as natural succession

can limit the growth of wild lupine and therefore limit the populations of Karner Blues and Frosted Elfins. Suppression of natural fires in the past has also reduced the number of open acres where lupines could grow.

The Ministry of Natural Resources is now working to control succession in the area by tree cutting and burning, to open up the habitat for lupines and the butterflies. In addition to these efforts, Lambton Wildlife Incorporated, a local naturalist group from Sarnia was able to purchase a tract of land in Lambton County, Ontario where Karner Blues were present. Their purchase, made possible with the help of the Ontario Heritage Foundation, will be a very important step in saving this butterfly.

Collection of rare butterflies is also a problem. Since they are difficult to find, they are highly sought after as very valuable "prize" specimens.

The widespread use of chemical pesticides, particularly in agriculture, has also affected some insect populations. Particularly in the past, many pesticides have been very broadly targetted, killing a wide variety of non-pest species along with one or two problem species.

Doing Something

It is important for students to understand how insects can be in jeopardy. But it is equally important that students learn what they can do to help.

Activities

1. Why should we care about insects becoming endangered or even extinct? By building a display/bulletin board, your class can answer that question for themselves. If possible, create the display in an area where the whole school can see it, so your students can play a role in educating their peers about insects.

Design a display or bulletin board with the heading "Hug a Bug — Insects are Important!"

From the following list, have students draw or find pictures that represent all the important contributions insects make to our society, as well as their own intrinsic values. Students can add their own ideas, as well.

— many insects are beautiful and a pleasure to watch

— insects are very important food sources for a variety of animals including birds, fish, reptiles, amphibians, spiders, other insects, mammals (shrews, bears, mice, skunks, etc. and even people)

— as a result of their importance in the food chain of some animals, insects are important to recreational pursuits such as fishing and birdwatching

— some insects, especially bees, are extremely valuable for their pollination activities; without them, the variety of flowering plants would be greatly reduced and many of our fruit and vegetable crops would not exist

— many commercial products come from insects, including honey, bees' wax, silk, shellac, tannin and various dyes

— some insects are widely used in laboratory research, particularly in genetic research; their short life cycles, high rate of reproduction, and ease of handling all lend themselves to research

— various medicines have been created using insect products such as tannic acid from insect galls and bee venom

— ground dwelling insects such as ants, various beetles, roaches, and earwigs are very important as soil mixers and aerators, improving plant growth

— many insects work as decomposers of dead plant and animal materials, releasing the stored nutrients back to the soil for plants to use

— some insects are, themselves, important pest controllers; for example, ladybird beetles control aphids and whiteflies on plants, and dragonflies eat mosquitoes; other insects have been used to control agricultural weeds

(The use of a plant or animal to control another plant or animal is called biocontrol. It has many potential benefits over the use of chemicals, including a more target specific control, no residues in the environment and the target cannot develop resistance to a natural predator as it can to a chemical pesticide. Biocontrol must be very carefully researched and monitored, however, to ensure that a species introduced to control a pest, does not itself become a pest. A lot of research is ongoing in the field of biocontrol and it is proving to be economically valuable where it has been used. It is hoped that an increased use of this insect control method will decrease society's current dependence on chemical pesticides.)

— many species we consider as pests in our artificial human environments, such as cockroaches and termites, play very important roles in "natural" environments such as rainforests and other tropical forests

2. There are many projects to help endangered species around the world. Conservation groups, governments, private companies and individuals have joined together to give money and expertise to help save a variety of species. For example, conservation groups are working to save vast tracts of tropical rainforests — home to thousands of insect species.

Students are not helpless. The problems may seem huge, but even young children can do their part to help endangered species. Here are a few ideas:

— Spread the word. The more people know about a problem, the more they'll care and want to help. Start a "bug club" at school and get together to go bugwatching. You can also put together insect awareness campaigns in your school or community.

— Invite guest speakers to the class to learn more. Contact your local zoo or museum or your local field naturalist club. Find out if there is an entomological society in your area.

— Support a group that is helping endangered species. You can give them money or volunteer your time. From bake sales to car washes to raffles, children all over the world are raising money for research and protection for wildlife.

— Write letters to governments about what you think should be done to help wildlife. Congratulate them on the work they are doing and suggest more ideas.

— Get involved in a community conservation project. Local groups can do very important work, so find out what's going on around you.

3. Have students role-play various characters in order to appreciate the different ways that insects are viewed in society. Divide the class into four groups. Assign each group one of the "situations" listed below, or make up your own. Within each group, individual students take on the roles listed and make up a short (5 minutes or so) skit to show everyone's point of view.

Ponds and marshes are being heavily sprayed by the local government to kill mosquitoes.

Roles:
— local government spokesperson
— head of local nature club
— someone who enjoys fishing
— birdwatcher
— local cottage owner in favor of spraying
— local cottage owner opposed to spraying

Construction of a new road through a woodlot threatens to destroy a population of rare butterflies.

Roles:
— head of local nature club
— president of construction company union
— biologist
— local politician in favor of new road
— local politician opposed to new road
— head of a local industry that will use new road

Farmer sprays orchard with chemicals to kill insect pests.

Roles:
— farmer who sprays orchard
— organic farmer
— person who buys fruit and supports spraying program
— person who buys fruit and opposes spraying program
— local birdwatcher
— person from fruit marketing board

A group of friends sitting around talking about their own attitudes toward insects.

Roles:
— person who sprays or kills every insect in sight just because it's an insect
— person who is totally against killing anything, including insects
— person who believes that some insect control is good, but most insects are harmless and should be left alone
— person concerned about environmental consequences of too much spraying and loss of insect populations
— person concerned about health effects of sprays on foodcrops and in recreational areas
— person concerned about a decline in the quality of food and an increase in food prices if insect pests are not controlled by chemicals
— person who is fascinated by insects and loves to study them

4. Creating an insect garden can be a great conservation activity for your class. With some cooperation from the groundskeeper at your school, you can plant some inviting plants for butterflies or bees and help out the local insect populations. Depending on your school yard, you can try growing plants in pots or in a small flower bed. Many schools have flower beds around the front doors. You may be able to get some space in these.

Your class can be responsible for watering and weeding your plants, or you can make arrangements with the caretaker. The students should, however, have some ongoing involvement in their project.

Once you've decided where to make your garden, decide what you want to attract. Bees or butterflies are fairly common and easily attracted.

Decide what you will plant. Bees are attracted by nectar-rich, fragrant flowers especially blue or purple ones, such as fuschia, clover, hyacinths, cosmos and snapdragons. Early spring-flowering bulbs such as crocuses are also valuable since they provide a food source when little else is available. Spring bulbs must be planted the previous fall. Butterflies can be attracted with parsley, carrots, and dill, as well as nectar-rich, flat-topped flowers. For maximum effectiveness, plant clumps of flowers, rather than single stems. Avoid insect-repelling flowers like marigolds or nasturtiums.

Share the planting jobs among your students. Some can till the garden or put the soil in the pots, others plant the seeds, others water, and others make and erect project signs that tell what the plants are.

Set up a monitoring system among your students to make sure the garden is prospering, to pick up litter, or fix vandalized parts, and to report on any signs of insect activity.

Student Activity Sheets

Insect Highlights

Insect Highlights

Meet An Insect

This insect has gone to pieces. Its basic body parts and their labels are all mixed up on this page. You need to cut out all the pieces and put them together on a separate sheet of paper, like a puzzle, to form a dragonfly.

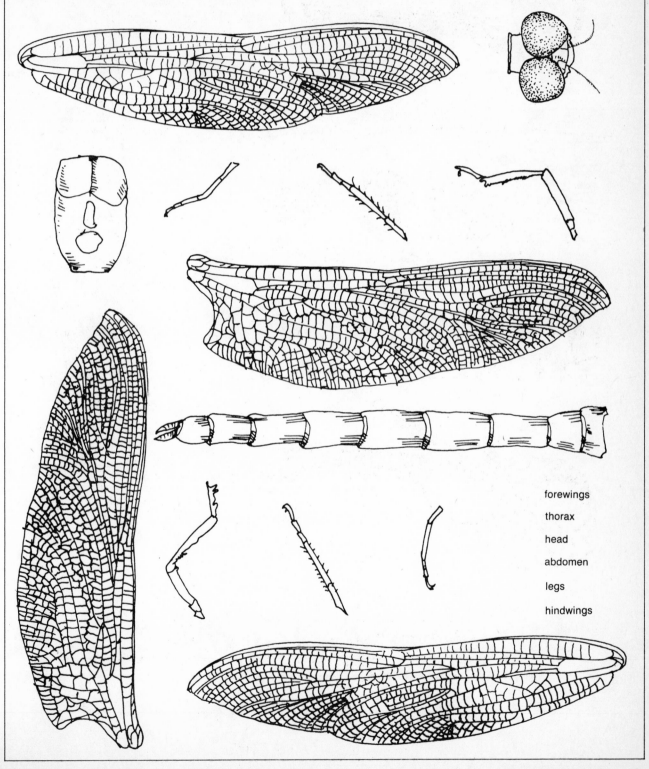

forewings

thorax

head

abdomen

legs

hindwings

Insect or Impostor?

Here is a variety of insects and non-insects. Put an ✓ in the box beside all the creatures you think are insects. Put an X in the box beside all the impostors.

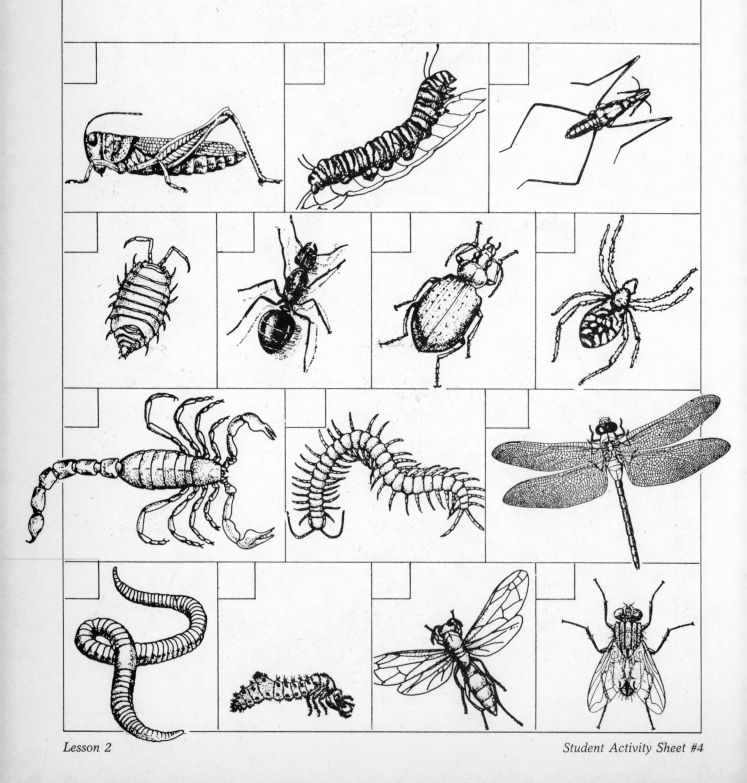

Stream Ecosystem

Stream Cutouts

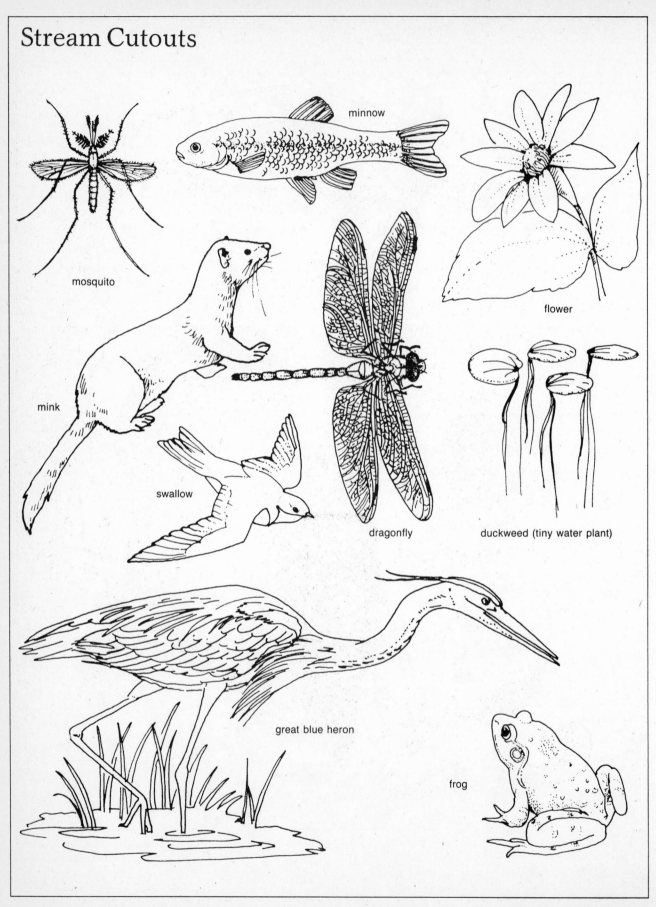

mosquito

minnow

flower

mink

dragonfly

duckweed (tiny water plant)

swallow

great blue heron

frog

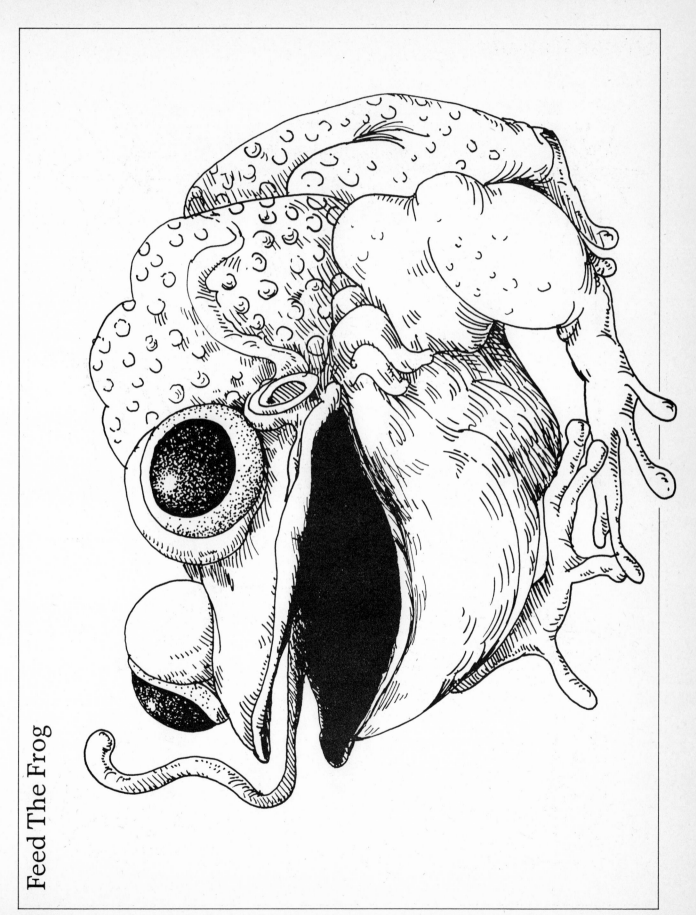

Feed The Frog

Feed the Frog

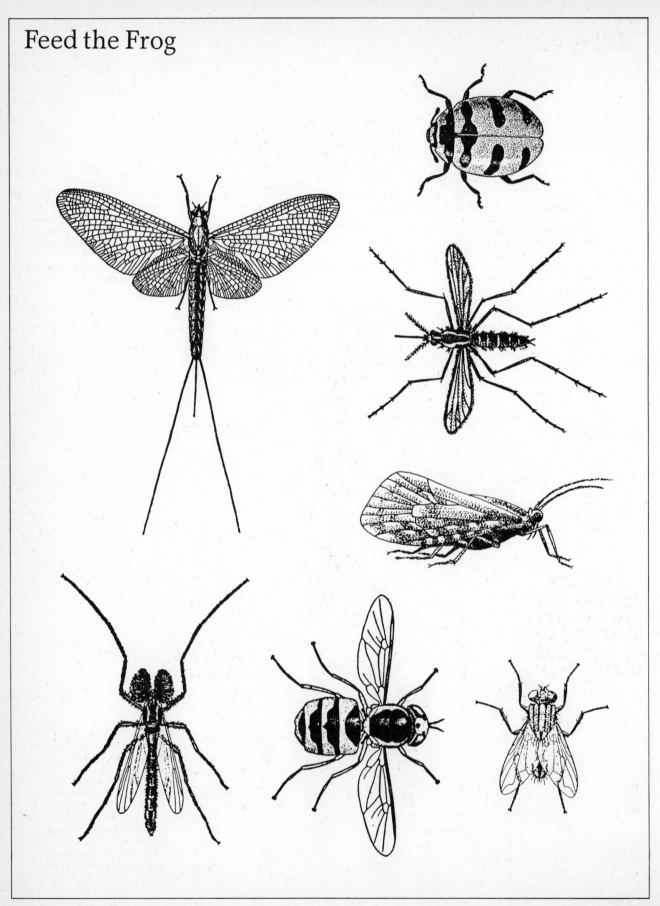

Killer Plants

Rolling Over (butterwort)
The flat, sticky leaves of the butterwort attract insects and then hold on tight. Once the insect is stuck to the leaf, the edges of the leaf roll inward to cover the insect. Inside the trap, the insect is eaten.

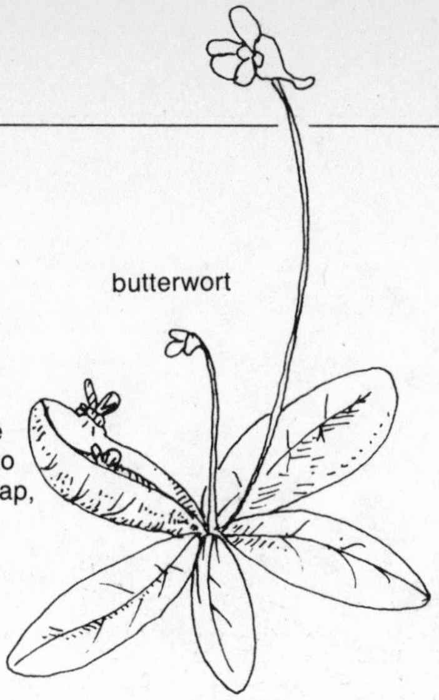

Clamming Up (Venus fly trap)
The Venus fly trap doesn't really come from the planet Venus — it only grows in North and South Carolina in the United States. It has hinged leaves, fringed with long bristles that are very sensitive to touch. When an insect brushes against the leaf, the leaf snaps shut, like a clam, trapping its dinner inside.

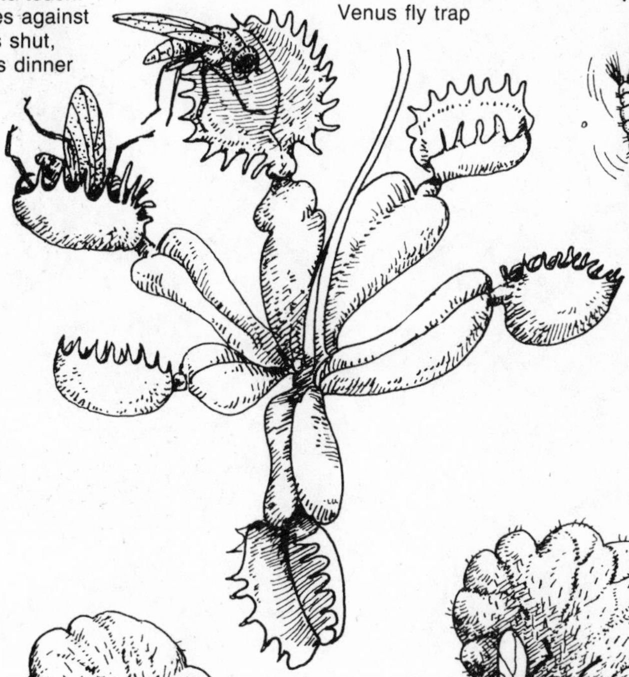

Sucking Up (bladderwort)
Bladderwort has little hollow pouches on its floating leaves, fringed with hairs. If a hair is touched, a trapdoor swings open, the pouch is blown up with air like a balloon, and the insect is sucked inside like a vacuum sucks up dirt.

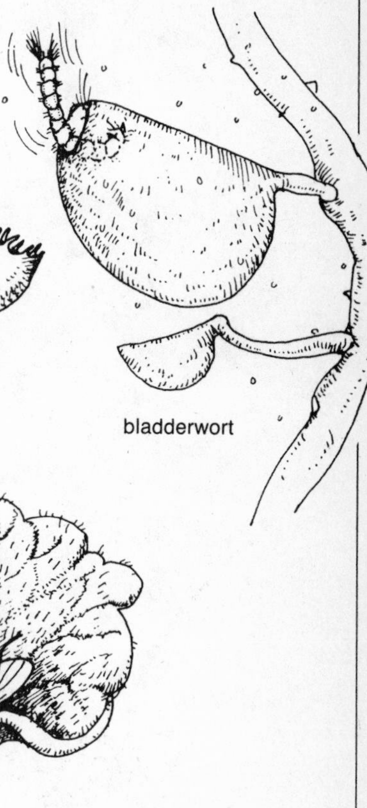

Venus fly trap

Sticking Down (sundew)
Sundews look like tiny red suns with long rays of hairs, tipped with dew drop-like glue. If you were an insect and landed on the sundew, you'd be stuck down on the hairs and wouldn't be able to get free. The hairy leaves would close over you like a temporary stomach and then you'd be eaten.

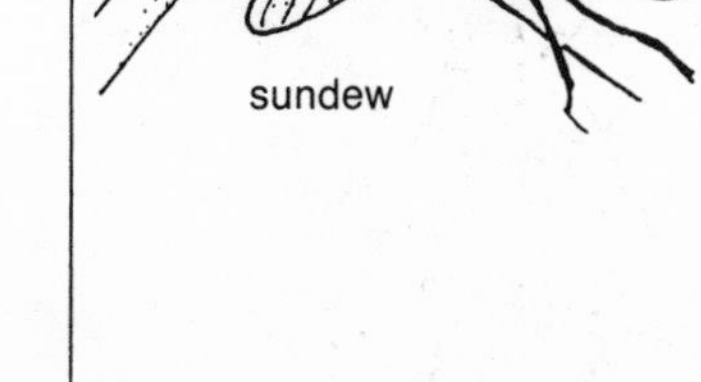

bladderwort

sundew

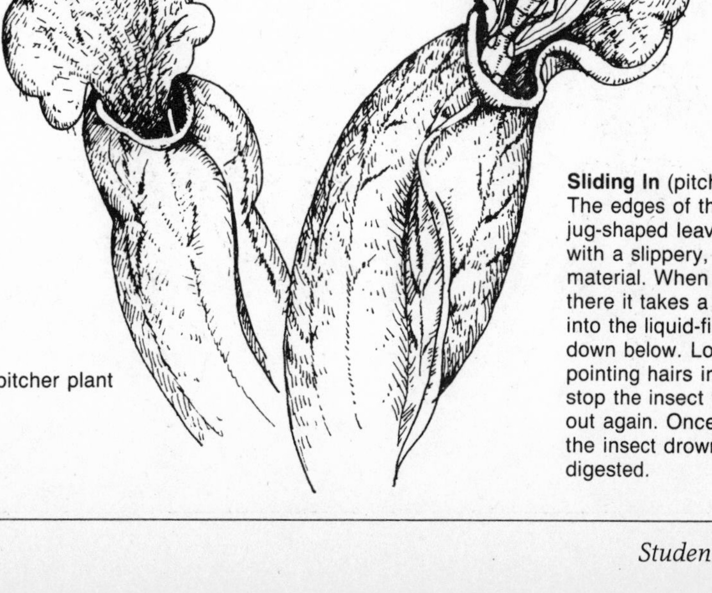

pitcher plant

Sliding In (pitcher plant)
The edges of the pitcher plant's jug-shaped leaves are coated with a slippery, wax-like material. When an insect lands there it takes a big slide, right into the liquid-filled pitcher down below. Long downward-pointing hairs inside the pitcher stop the insect from crawling out again. Once in the liquid, the insect drowns and is soon digested.

Busy Bee Maze

Help this bee get its pollen back to the hive. Use a pencil to trace its path. Try to visit as many flowers as possible on the way, without crossing any solid lines. How many flowers did the bee pollinate on the way back?

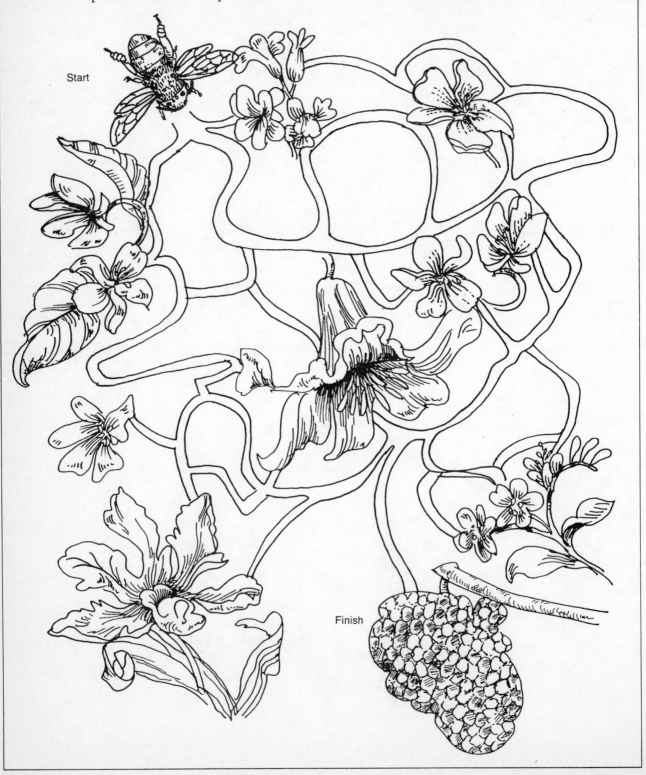

Start

Finish

The Better To Eat You

Some insects have special adaptations for catching their food. Their built-in "tools" sometimes remind us of objects in our world. Match the description of the seven insects with the appropriate human item illustrated.

1. A house fly would be great at cleaning up spills. It has a wide, fleshy tip on its mouthparts that can soak up liquids in a flash.

2. When a honeybee is thirsty, it just pokes its tube-like mouthparts into the center of a flower, and sucks up the sweet nectar.

3. A long tube-like mouth can be awkward to carry around, so when moths and butterflies aren't drinking, they roll up their mouthparts to keep them out of the way.

4. Mosquitoes don't actually bite. They pierce your skin with their sharply pointed mouthparts, and suck up your blood.

5. The large front legs of the praying mantis are well equipped with pincers for grabbing and holding on to prey.

6. Dragonflies have long, thin legs edged with stiff bristles. When flying, their legs are folded beneath the body to form a trap for catching small flying insects.

7. The hind legs of most bees are large and covered with long, stiff hairs. The hairs are used to collect pollen and help carry large balls of pollen from the flowers, back to the hive.

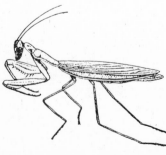

Aquatic Insects

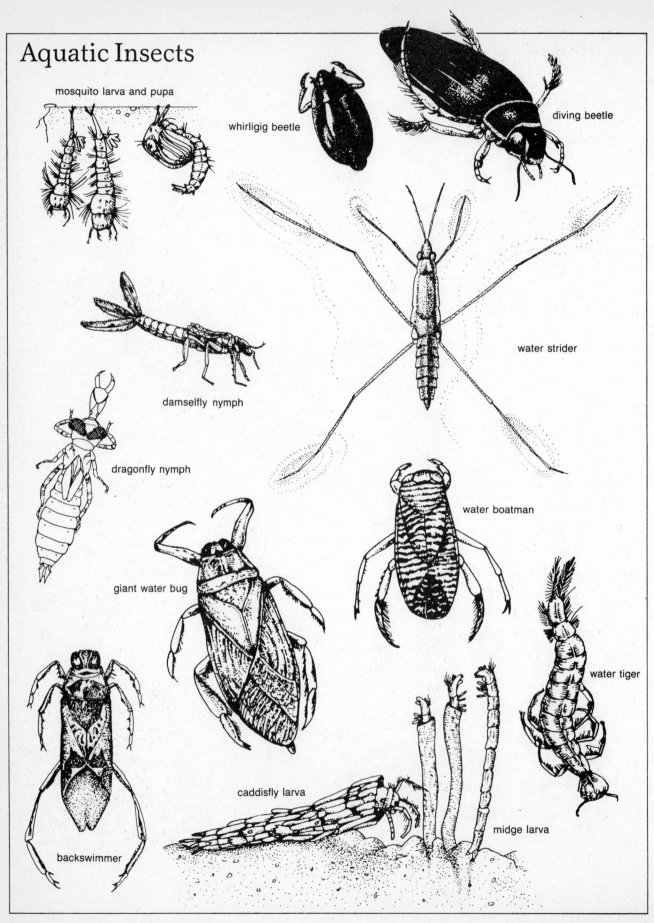

mosquito larva and pupa

whirligig beetle

diving beetle

damselfly nymph

water strider

dragonfly nymph

water boatman

giant water bug

water tiger

backswimmer

caddisfly larva

midge larva

Finders Keepers

Pretend you're a hungry bird looking for lunch. Try to find and circle all eight (8) of the hidden insects in this picture.

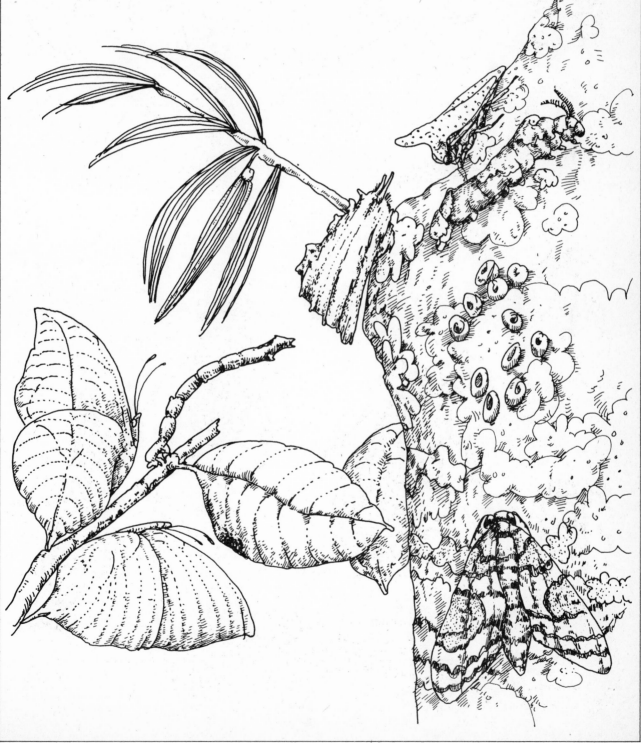

Bouncing Butterflies

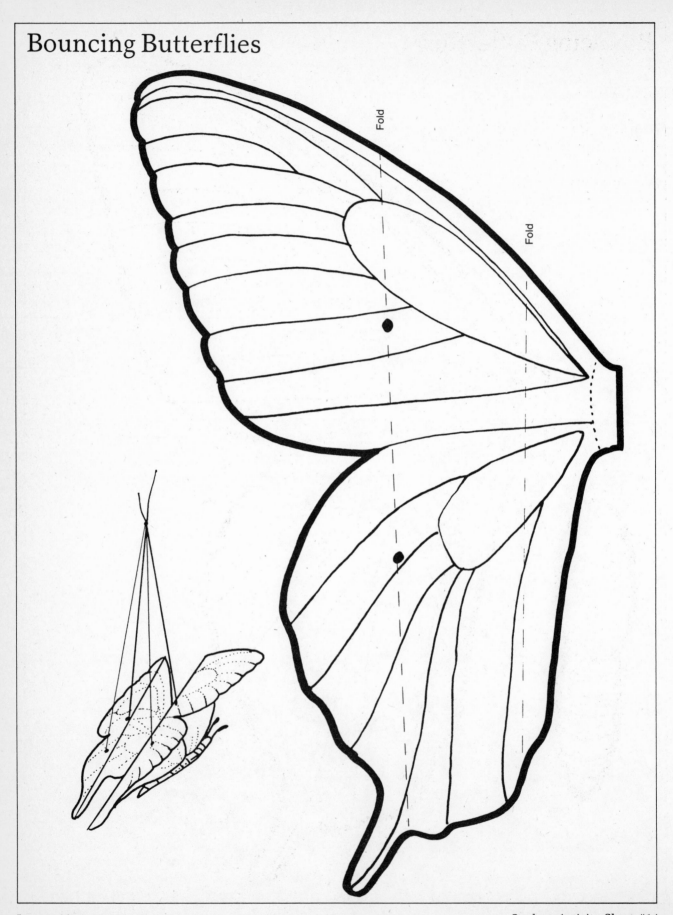

Fold

Fold

Bouncing Butterflies

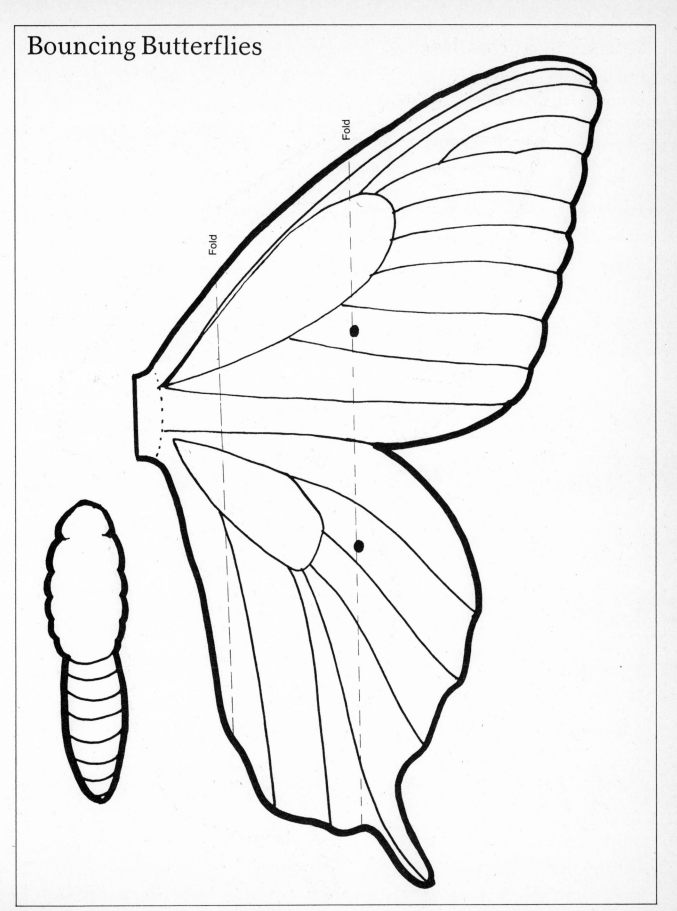

Fold

Fold

Counting on Jumps

Using the information in this chart, answer
the questions.

Insect	Distance jumped in one jump
springtail	20 cm (8")
flea	30 cm (12")
grasshopper	75 cm (30")
field cricket	60 cm (24")
flea beetle	25 cm (10")

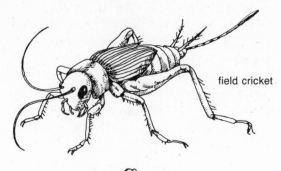

field cricket

1. Which insect jumped the third longest
   distance?

   _____

   _____

   _____

2. List the insect jumpers in order from
   longest jumper to shortest jumper.

   _____

   _____

   _____

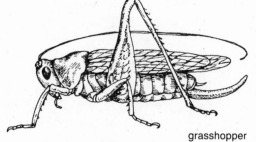

grasshopper

3. A grasshopper is 5 cm long and jumps
   75 cm. A flea is .15 cm long and jumps
   30 cm. Which insect is the better jumper
   and why?

   _____

   _____

   _____

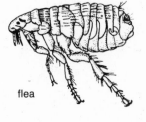

flea

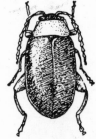

4. Have a partner measure how far you can
   jump from a standing position. Then
   measure how high you can jump.
   Compare these distances to your own
   height. A flea can jump 200 times its own
   body length. How do you compare? List
   some things that people use to help them
   jump farther or higher.

flea beetle

springtail

   _____

   _____

   _____

Crawling Caterpillars

— Fold the felt into a tube with the rounded
  edge at the top. Overlap the sides.
— Glue along the whole side and rounded
  top, leaving the bottom open. Press
  together until dry.
— Use felt scraps to make eyes on the head
  (rounded part).
— Use felt, wool, and sequins to decorate.

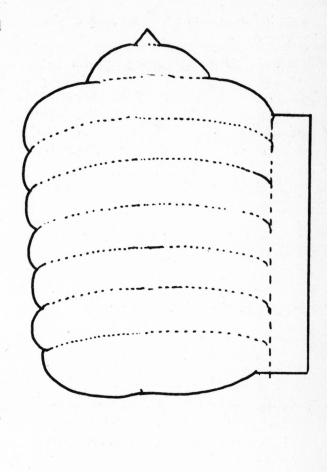

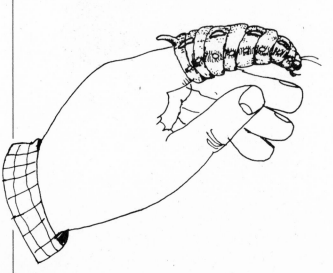

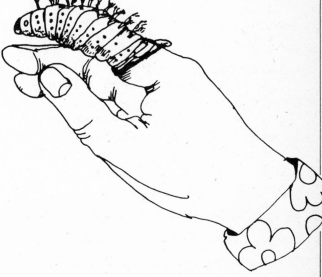

Feel Free

Let your fingers, face, and feet tell you what to say about different substances.

Write down your words to describe how the different things felt to you, e.g. sticky, soft, hard.

Fingers

Sample #1 _____

Sample #2 _____

Sample #3 _____

Sample #4 _____

Face

Sample #1 _____

Sample #2 _____

Sample #3 _____

Sample #4 _____

Feet

Sample #1 _____

Sample #2 _____

Sample #3 _____

Sample #4 _____

An Insect's Eye View

Look at the pictures below. On the left is a picture of a flower as you would see it. On the right is the same flower, drawn as an insect sees it. In the space below, draw a simple object as you see it. Beside your drawing, show the same object as an insect sees it. Label your drawings.

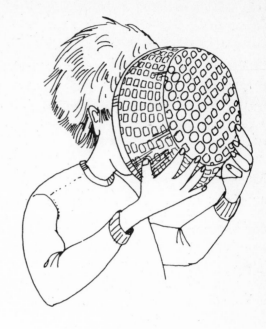

how a person sees a flower

how an insect sees a flower

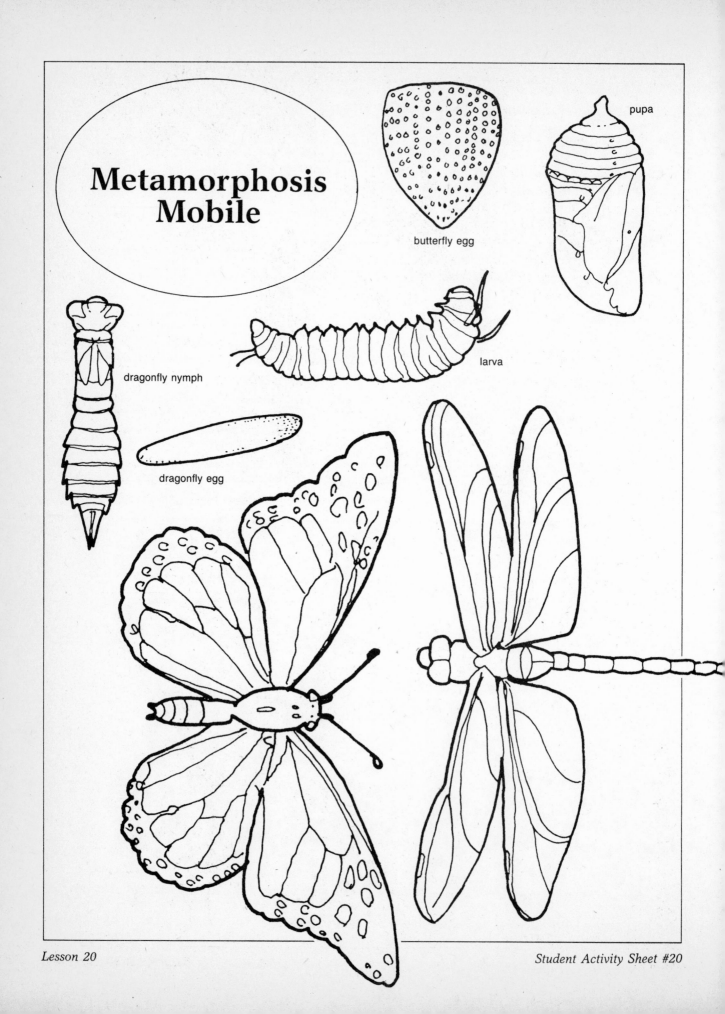

Metamorphosis Mobile

butterfly egg

pupa

dragonfly nymph

larva

dragonfly egg

Meet a Mosquito

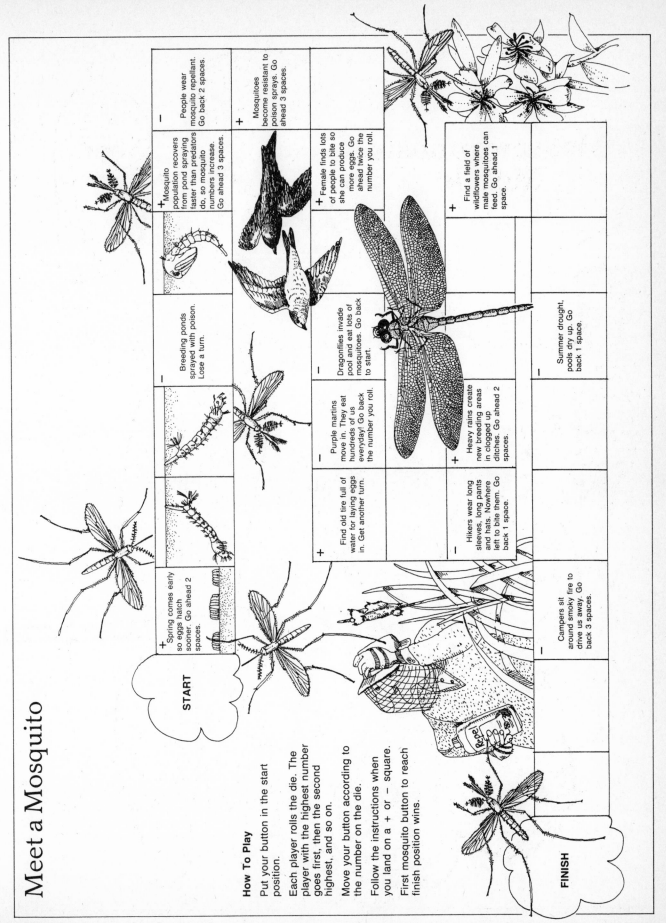

How To Play

Put your button in the start position.

Each player rolls the die. The player with the highest number goes first, then the second highest, and so on.

Move your button according to the number on the die.

Follow the instructions when you land on a + or – square.

First mosquito button to reach finish position wins.

START

FINISH

+ Spring comes early so eggs hatch sooner. Go ahead 2 spaces.

– Find old tire full of water for laying eggs in. Get another turn.

– Breeding ponds sprayed with poison. Lose a turn.

+ Mosquito population recovers from pond spraying faster than predators do, so mosquito numbers increase. Go ahead 3 spaces.

– People wear mosquito repellant. Go back 2 spaces.

+ Mosquitoes become resistant to poison sprays. Go ahead 3 spaces.

+ Female finds lots of people to bite so she can produce more eggs. Go ahead twice the number you roll.

+ Find a field of wildflowers where male mosquitoes can feed. Go ahead 1 space.

– Purple martins move in. They eat hundreds of us everyday! Go back the number you roll.

– Dragonflies invade pool and eat lots of mosquitoes. Go back to start.

+ Heavy rains create new breeding areas in clogged up ditches. Go ahead 2 spaces.

– Summer drought, pools dry up. Go back 1 space.

+ Hikers wear long sleeves, long pants and hats. Nowhere left to bite them. Go back 1 space.

– Campers sit around smoky fire to drive us away. Go back 3 spaces.

Winter Insect Hike

Mini-Guide to Hibernating Insects

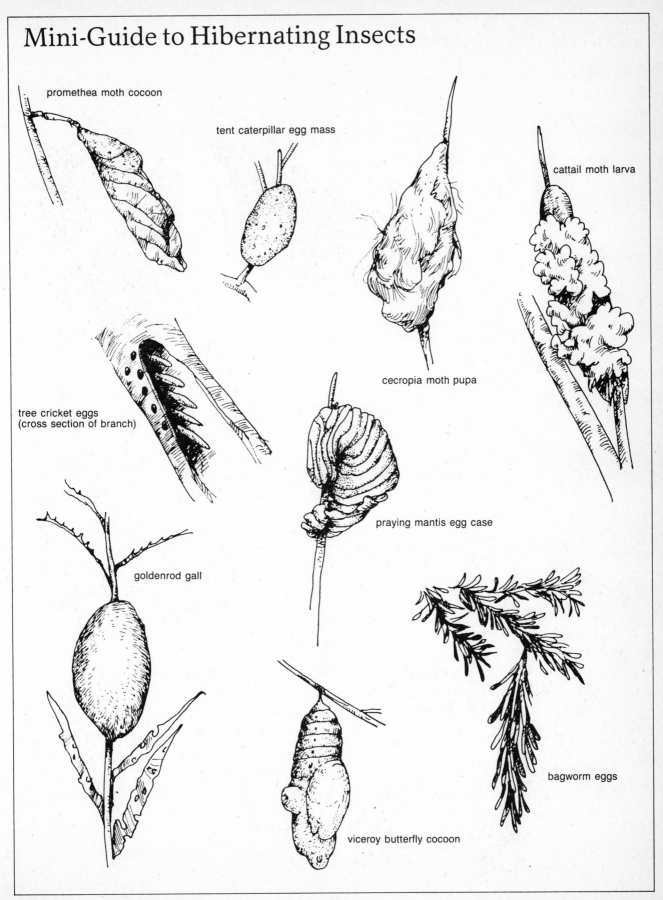

promethea moth cocoon

tent caterpillar egg mass

cattail moth larva

cecropia moth pupa

tree cricket eggs
(cross section of branch)

praying mantis egg case

goldenrod gall

bagworm eggs

viceroy butterfly cocoon

Insects In Code

Try to figure out the following names of insects that you might find on a winter insect hike. The insect names are written in a secret code. Here is a clue to help you crack the code. Each letter of the alphabet equals a number; A = 1, B = 2, C = 3, etc. So the code 2, 21, 7 would actually mean B, U, G. Write your answers in the spaces provided below each clue. Good luck!

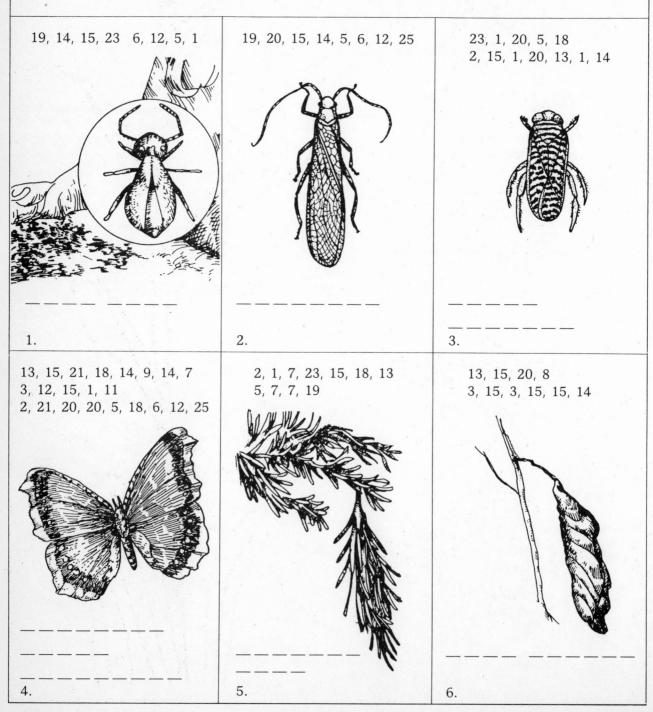

1. 19, 14, 15, 23 6, 12, 5, 1

_ _ _ _ _ _ _ _

2. 19, 20, 15, 14, 5, 6, 12, 25

_ _ _ _ _ _ _ _

3. 23, 1, 20, 5, 18
2, 15, 1, 20, 13, 1, 14

_ _ _ _ _
_ _ _ _ _ _ _

4. 13, 15, 21, 18, 14, 9, 14, 7
3, 12, 15, 1, 11
2, 21, 20, 20, 5, 18, 6, 12, 25

_ _ _ _ _ _ _ _
_ _ _ _ _
_ _ _ _ _ _ _ _ _

5. 2, 1, 7, 23, 15, 18, 13
5, 7, 7, 19

_ _ _ _ _ _ _
_ _ _ _

6. 13, 15, 20, 8
3, 15, 3, 15, 15, 14

_ _ _ _ _ _ _ _ _ _

Flower Feeders

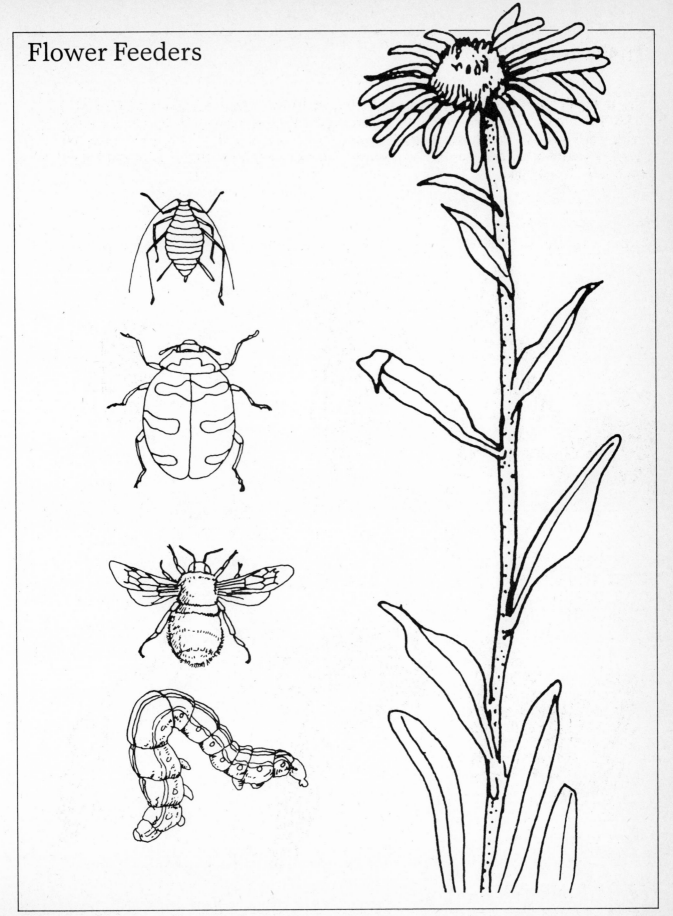

Feasting On Flowers

Circle the insects; put a colored circle around the insect eaters.

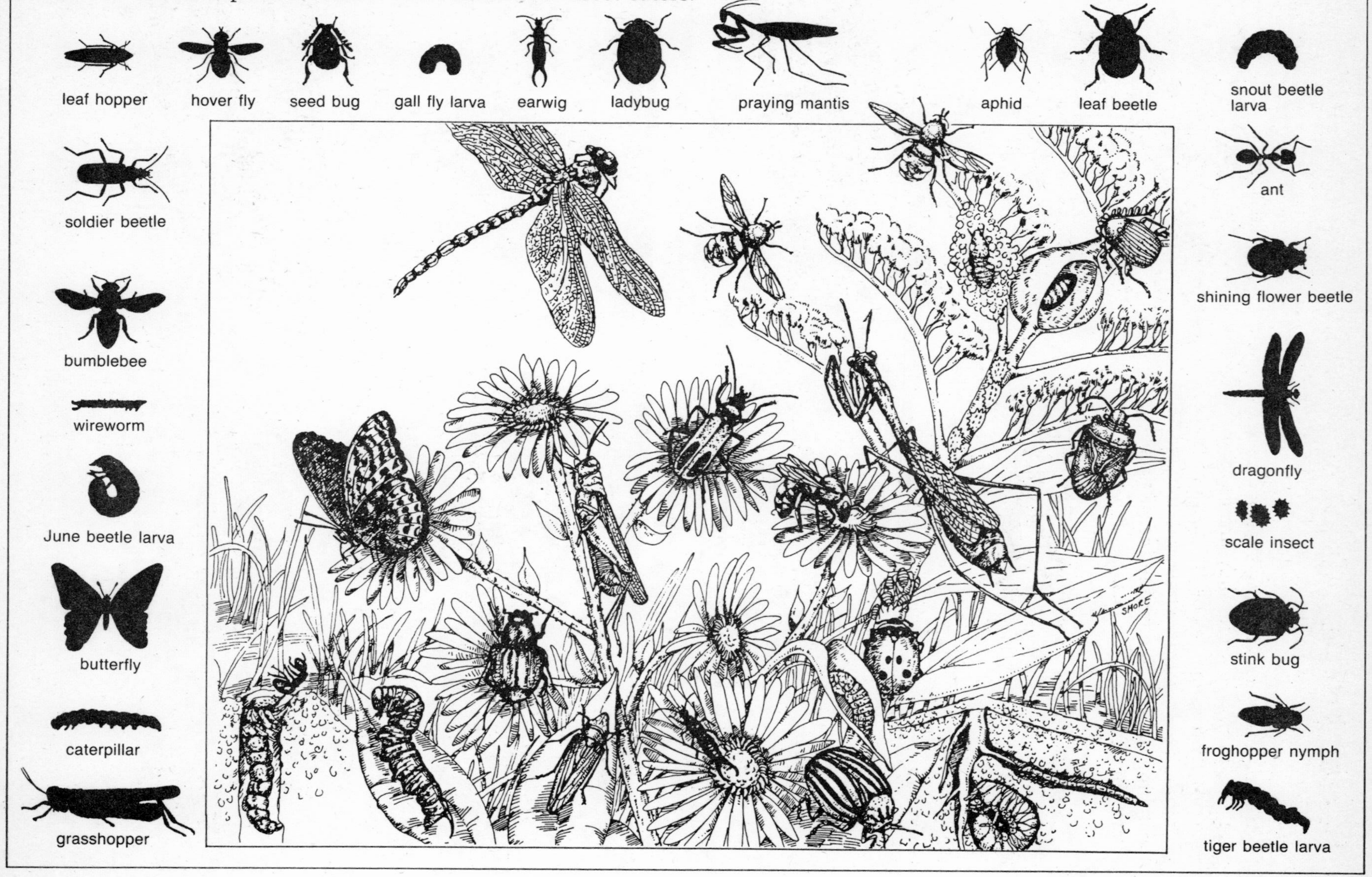

snout beetle larva

ant

shining flower beetle

dragonfly

scale insect

stink bug

froghopper nymph

tiger beetle larva

leaf beetle

aphid

praying mantis

ladybug

earwig

gall fly larva

seed bug

hover fly

leaf hopper

soldier beetle

bumblebee

wireworm

June beetle larva

butterfly

caterpillar

grasshopper

Insect Artists

Some insects make amazing shapes or patterns in nature while they are feeding or making their homes. Look for signs of these common insect artists while you are insect watching outside. Match the insect to its "art" by reading the clues.

1. I make big tunnels and chambers in dead wood where I lay my eggs and raise my family.
Who am I?

_____

2. The winding patterns you see on old stumps and rotting logs are my work. I engrave my lovely pictures on the wood while I travel around, eating.
Who am I?

_____

3. I can take an ordinary plant stem and make it much more interesting by adding big egg-shaped decorations to it.
Who am I?

_____

4. My delicate patterns are made in leaves. By eating as I move, I create pretty leaf pictures that show where I've been.
Who am I?

_____

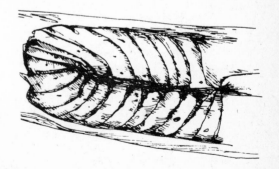

Hunting For Insects At Home

The following insects may be found even in the tidiest house. Try to find the insect names written inside this house. They may be written up or down, frontwards or backwards, or even diagonally! Circle your answers. We've circled the first one to get you started.

Look for these home-loving insects:
fruit fly
house fly
ladybug
cricket
ant
aphid
booklice
bee
earwig
moth

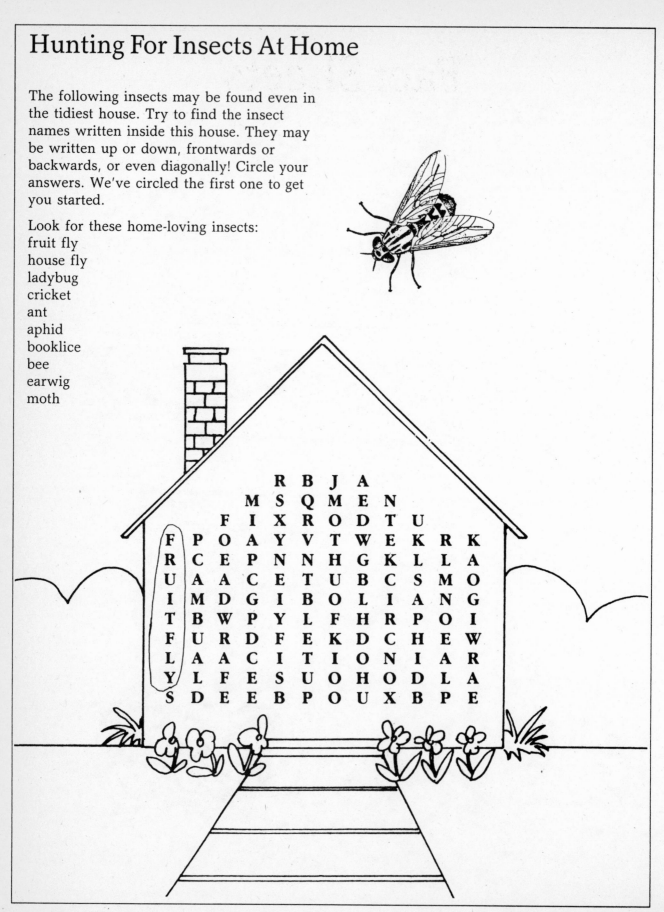

Fact Sheets

Ant

Order: *Hymenoptera*
Related Insects: bees, wasps, icheneumons, sawflies

Look at Me
— two long antennae
— often has a large head
— usually no wings (unmated queens and males have wings at certain times of year)
— small, narrow section at beginning of abdomen, often with one or two humps

Find Me
— different kinds of ants are found everywhere on land except the polar regions
— our most common ants live in underground burrows and rotting wood
— you've probably seen lots of ant hills between cracks in the sidewalk or in your lawn. These hills are a sign that ants have built a home below ground.

Let's Eat
— ants eat a variety of foods: some dine on plant juices, leaves, seeds and fungus, some eat other insects, and of course, you are probably familiar with those that scrounge your crumbs at picnics
— some ants actually act like farmers, "herding and milking" aphids (another kind of insect) the way a farmer milks a cow. The aphids give off droplets of a sweet liquid called honeydew that the ants quickly lick up.

My Life Story
— ants are social insects. This means that they live in a colony with thousands of other ants, working together and relying on each other.
— ants are divided into queens, males and workers (sterile females)
— there is usually just one queen per colony (although some species will have more than one) and it is her job to lay all the eggs. The workers do all the chores in the colony, including cleaning, nursing the young, feeding the queen and defending the colony from danger.
— every fall a group of ants with wings is born. These are new queens and males. They leave the colony and mate. The males die soon after mating, but each queen finds a new home and starts her own colony.
— ants undergo complete metamorphosis. This means that they have four life stages: egg, larva, pupa, adult.

I'm Special
— there are more ants, with respect to biomass, than any other creature on earth
— ants can lift up to 50 times their own weight. That's like your lifting two small cars!
— ants speak using smells, not sounds. By giving off certain chemical odours, one ant can tell another who it is, where it has just been and whether or not there is food around.
— ants are among the smartest of all insects

P.S.
— you can lure ants out of their underground nest by sprinkling some sugar-covered bread crumbs near the ant-hill. Watch the ants try to carry the crumbs back to their burrow. You will soon see how well these social insects can cooperate to get a job done.

Words to Learn
— abdomen, complete metamorphosis, larva, pupa, social insect, sterile

Dragonfly

Order: *Odonata*
Related Insects: damselflies

Look at Me
— adult has a long, slender body, often brightly colored
— 4 long, usually clear, shiny wings. Hind wings are slightly larger than forewings. Sometimes there are black or white colorations on the wings of some local species.
— wings covered with lots of veins
— very large compound eyes, sometimes touching together in the middle
— 6 long, slender legs

Find Me
— adults are found flying around water such as ponds, streams and marshes
— often seen resting on the reeds or other plants growing in the water
— when at rest, a dragonfly's wings are always held out straight, never folded over its back
— nymphs are aquatic, swimming underwater

Let's Eat
— everyone likes adult dragonflies because they eat so many mosquitoes, as well as other small flying insects
— they fold their legs under their bodies in a basket-like shape and then scoop mosquitoes out of the air
— they have chewing mouthparts
— dragonfly nymphs are big eaters — even attacking small fish. They have an amazing jaw that is hinged on one side of the nymph's head. When food is near, the jaw swings out like a robot's arm, grabs the prey, and brings it back to the mouth.

My Life Story
— dragonflies undergo incomplete metamorphosis. That means they have only three stages in their lives: egg, nymph and adult.
— eggs are laid on plants in the water and hatch into nymphs
— as nymphs grow, they shed their "skin" (called moulting), revealing a new, larger "skin" below the old one
— dragonfly nymphs often take two years before turning into adults
— a nymph crawls up on a plant stem out of the water and sits very still
— in a few hours its "skin" will split along its back and the adult will climb out, leaving the ghost-like shell of the nymph's body still attached to the stem
— the adult unfolds its wings, flaps them so they'll dry, and pumps fluid through the wings' veins to expand and strengthen the wings
— the adult now flies away

I'm Special
— dragonflies are the fastest fliers in the marsh, reaching speeds of 40 km/h (60 mph)
— dragonflies are important natural controllers of mosquitoes
— dragonfly nymphs have a great way to get around in the water — jet propulsion. A nymph can shoot water out of its abdomen with such force that it will take off with a spurt, leaving an enemy far behind.

P.S.
— here's an easy way to tell the difference between a dragonfly and its look-alike, the damselfly: damselflies fold their wings up over their backs when resting, but a dragonfly's wings are always stretched out flat
— dragonflies are sometimes called mosquito hawks

Words to Learn
aquatic, incomplete metamorphosis, moult, nymph

Mosquito

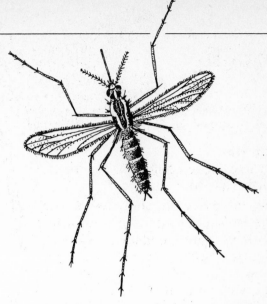

Order: *Diptera*
Related Insects: flies, midges, gnats

Look at Me
— adult has 2 long, narrow, clear wings
— 6 long, thin legs
— 2 long, sometimes feathery (in males) antennae
— long, pointed mouthpart called a proboscis (pro-boss-is)

Find Me
— adults are found in just about any habitat
— eggs, larvae and pupae are all found in water, especially still water like ditches, small ponds, meltpools or even old containers filled with rainwater

Let's Eat
— you probably know what female mosquitoes eat — your blood! The proteins in your blood help the females produce their eggs. When a mosquito bites you, it pierces your skin with its needle-like proboscis. It then spits saliva into the wound, to stop your blood from clotting (forming a scab), so she can get a good drink.
— male mosquitoes (along with females) suck flower nectar with their straw-like mouthparts and therefore play a role in flower pollination
— mosquito larvae feed mostly on bits of plant material in the water
— pupae don't feed at all

My Life Story
— mosquitoes undergo complete metamorphosis. That means they have four life stages: egg, larva, pupa, adult.
— the eggs are laid on the surface of the water, sometimes in clumps called rafts

— larvae, called wrigglers, live just beneath the water's surface, usually breathing through an air tube on their abdomen
— unlike many insect pupae, mosquito pupae are active in the water. They live just below the surface, looking like small, dark commas hanging in the water.
— when the adult is ready to come out, the back of the pupa's "skin" splits and the adult climbs out onto the water's surface. It quickly expands its wings and flies off.

I'm Special
— mosquitoes are a very important food source for other animals, including fish, frogs, toads, turtles and many birds
— some mosquitoes, mainly in tropical areas, carry diseases such as yellow fever and malaria
— one species of mosquito larva eats other mosquito larva and is a great mosquito control in the tropics

P.S.
— if you want to avoid too many mosquito bites this summer, try wearing long sleeves, long pants and a hat when out in "mosquito country". Light-colored clothing is best.
— use rub-on insect repellants instead of aerosol sprays

Words to Learn
complete metamorphosis, larva, nectar, proboscis, protein, pupa

Ladybird Beetle (Ladybug)

nine-spotted ladybug

Order: *Coleoptera*
Related Insects: all beetles

Look at Me
— adult has a roundish to oval body
— orange, yellowish or reddish body with black spots
— 6 black legs
— like all beetles, the ladybird has two pairs of wings. The front pair is modified into hard, protective coverings, called elytra, which lie over the thin hind wings. The hard wings not only protect the thin wings, but also the insect's soft body. When resting, the ladybug folds its hind pair of wings underneath the elytra. When flying, the hard wings are held up and out of the way.

three-banded ladybug

confused convergent ladybug

My Life Story
— all beetles undergo complete metamorphosis. That is, they have four life stages: egg, larva, pupa, adult.
— the tiny oval, yellow eggs are laid in clumps on the underside of leaves
— the small black and orange larvae spend their time feeding on insects before turning into pupae
— ladybugs spend winter as adults, often in large groups below the leaf litter

I'm Special
— ladybugs are very important to farmers because they eat many insects that are harmful to plants, including orchard crops. In fact, ladybugs imported from Australia were responsible for saving the California citrus orange crops.
— there are over 5000 different kinds of ladybugs and over 290 000 different kinds of beetles in the world!

Find Me
— ladybugs are usually found on plants in gardens and fields or in leaf litter on the ground
— adults of the two-spotted ladybug often spend winters inside buildings and may be found at windows in the fall or spring.

Let's Eat
— most adult and larval ladybird beetles feed on harmful plant pests such as aphids, scale insects and mites
— ladybirds, like all beetles, have chewing mouthparts

P.S.
— Has anyone ever told you that you can tell a ladybug's age by counting its spots? It's not true. The number of spots tells you what kind of ladybug it is, not how old it is.

Words to Learn
complete metamorphosis, elytra, larva, leaf litter, pupa

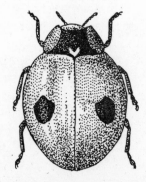

two-spotted ladybug

Monarch Butterfly

Order: *Lepidoptera*
Related Insects: butterflies, moths

Look at Me
— black body
— adult has 4 large, black and orange wings
— two long antennae with small knobs on the ends

Find Me
— adult monarchs can be found in open areas such as parks, fields and gardens
— eggs, larvae, and pupae are found on milkweed plants in open fields or roadsides

Let's Eat
— larvae feed with their well-developed chewing mouthparts on milkweed leaves
— adults have a long thin tube for a mouth. It is used for drinking flower nectar. When not in use, the tube is coiled up below the head, like a party blower.

My Life Story
— butterflies go through 4 life stages, a process called complete metamorphosis. The stages are: egg, larva (caterpillar), pupa (chrysalis), and adult
— adult monarchs lay their tiny hive-shaped eggs on the underside of milkweed leaves
— when the yellow, white, and black striped caterpillars hatch out, they begin to eat the leaves. The caterpillars grow very quickly and will reach 2700 times their original size in just a couple of weeks!
— caterpillars have special silk glands in their abdomens. Before forming a chrysalis, the monarch caterpillar spins a silk pad on a leaf or branch, attaches its abdomen to the pad and then hangs upside down in a J-shape.
— gradually the larva's stripes fade and an emerald green pupa, or chrysalis is formed. After a couple of days, golden droplets appear on the chrysalis.
— inside the chrysalis, the adult is being formed. After 9-10 days, the chrysalis' green color fades and the pupal case becomes clear, like a window. The black and orange adult is now visible.
— within two weeks of forming the chrysalis splits open, releasing the adult.
— after drying its wings and pumping liquid through the wings' veins, the adult is ready to fly
— males can be told from females by looking for black spots on the hind wings

I'm Special
— people have about 639 muscles in their bodies. How many do you think a tiny caterpillar has? The answer is over 4000! Caterpillars need lots of different muscles to help them crawl around.
— Monarch butterflies are famous for their long migrations. In the fall, huge flocks of monarchs leave southern Canada and head for the southern United States and Central America. In late winter they start back northward, but stop on the way to lay eggs. It is the butterflies raised from these eggs that continue the journey back to Canada in the spring.

P.S.
— Can you tell a butterfly from a moth?
  a) butterflies have knobs at the ends of their antennae but a moth's antennae are threadlike or feathery
  b) a moth's body tends to be fatter and hairier than a butterfly's body
  c) butterflies fly during the day, but most moths are night fliers
  d) when resting, butterflies close their wings high over their backs but moths can fold their wings down on top of their backs
  e) the pupa of a butterfly forms a smooth chrysalis, but a moth pupa usually spins a cocoon of silk

Words to Learn
abdomen, chrysalis, cocoon, complete metamorphosis, larva, migration, pupa

Common Flea

Order: *Siphonaptera*

Look at Me
— very small
— flattened from side to side
— no wings
— 6 long legs

Find Me
— most commonly found living on the skin and in the hair of pets such as dogs and cats
— because the flea is flattened from side to side it moves easily between the animal's hairs and is very hard to catch
— fleas often move from one host to another, and can also be found in a pet's bed or wherever it normally rests

Let's Eat
— fleas have sucking mouthparts and feed on the blood of their hosts by piercing their skin

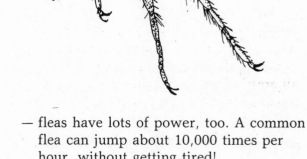

My Life Story
— fleas undergo complete metamorphosis, with four life stages: egg, larva, pupa and adult
— eggs are laid in dirt, or the nest or bedding of the host (such as a dog's bed). Sometimes eggs are laid on the host and then fall off into its bedding.
— larvae are whitish, legless creatures with large heads and two small hooks on the ends of their bodies
— pupae form in silken cocoons

I'm Special
— fleas are amazing athletes, able to jump 200 times their own body length in one bound. That's like a person jumping five city blocks!

— fleas have lots of power, too. A common flea can jump about 10,000 times per hour, without getting tired!

P.S.
— fleas can be very annoying pests for pets, as well as people who may also be bitten
— some fleas carry diseases such as plague. Fleas are species specific. This means that each species feeds on one food type — dogs, cats, rodents, rabbits, birds etc.

Words to Learn
cocoon, complete metamorphosis, larva, pupa

Grasshopper

Order: *Orthoptera*
Related Insects: crickets, katydids

Look at Me
— 2 pairs of wings
— large head
— very large hind legs for jumping
— 2 long antennae
— long body

Find Me
— fields of long grass, unmown ditches, roadsides

Let's Eat
— grasshoppers eat plants and several species can cause problems for farmers by eating their field crops
— all grasshoppers have chewing mouthparts

My Life Story
— since grasshoppers have only three life stages — egg, nymph and adult — they undergo incomplete metamorphosis
— eggs are laid in the ground in the fall and stay there all winter long. When the warm weather returns, the eggs hatch and the tiny nymphs appear.
— a nymph looks very similar to the adult, although it is usually wingless. As the nymph grows, it sheds its skin to make more room for its growing body. Each stage of moulting is called an instar. Most grasshopper nymphs go through at least 5 instars.
— when the nymph is finished growing it moults into its adult form

I'm Special
— grasshoppers are one of the "musical" insects, making a very familiar chirping sound in the long grass

— they produce their music sort of like a person playing the violin. Short-horned grasshoppers have a row of bumps, known as a file, on their hind legs. The file is rubbed against the scraper, a ridge on the forewing, just like the bow of a violin is drawn across the strings.
— it's usually the males that "sing", trying to attract a mate
— grasshoppers are amazing jumpers. Their strong hind legs help them jump 75 cm in one leap. That's the same as your covering one-third the length of a football field in one jump!

P.S.
— the snowy tree cricket is related to grasshoppers. It is called a "living thermometer" because if you count the number of chirps it produces in 8 seconds and then add 4, you can get the approximate temperature in degrees Celsius!

Words to Learn
incomplete metamorphosis, instar, moult, nymph

Caddisfly

Order: *Trichoptera*

Look at Me
— adult has 2 very long thread-like antennae
— slender, long, brownish body
— 2 pairs of wings folded up over its back
— looks a bit like a moth

Find Me
— adults are widely spread, spending the days resting in cool, dark places and flying at night. Adults are often attracted to lights at night.
— larvae and pupae are aquatic (a-kwa-tic), living in ponds and streams

Let's Eat
— larvae have chewing mouthparts and most feed on plants. Some build tiny silken nets to strain food out of the water as the water flows through the net.
— some species of larvae feed on other insects and are important for eating large numbers of black flies
— most adults have sucking mouthparts for drinking fluids, but some adults do not feed at all

My Life Story
— caddisflies undergo complete metamorphosis, with four life stages: egg, larva, pupa, adult
— the eggs are laid in strings or clumps on stones, plants or other materials in or near the water
— the larvae look a bit like caterpillars, but have gills on their abdomens for breathing
— caddisfly larvae are very interesting because many species build themselves tiny cases or armour out of bits of sticks, leaves or stones, held together with silk or a gluelike material
— when the larva is finished growing it attaches its case to a stone or other object in the water, seals the case and pupates inside

— the pupa chews its way out of the case, crawls out of the water onto a stone and moults into an adult

I'm Special
— caddisfly larvae can be found crawling around in the shallows of streams and ponds. Their little cases are amazing constructions and help hide them from predators. They sometimes look just like a little stick or clump of stones crawling along all by themselves. Different species make different cases.

P.S.
— caddisflies, especially the larvae and pupae, are a very important food source for many freshwater fish

Words to Learn
abdomen, aquatic, complete metamorphosis, larva, moult, predator, pupa

Water Strider

Order: *Hemiptera*
Related Insects: water boatman, backswimmer, stink bug, leaf bug and other bugs

Look at Me
— long, thin body
— front legs short, but other four legs are very long and thin
— some have wings, while others are wingless
— 2 long antennae

Find Me
— found on the surface of ponds and slow streams

Let's Eat
— adults feed on small insects that fall onto the surface of the water
— all insects in this order have sucking mouthparts

My Life Story
— like all true bugs, water striders undergo incomplete metamorphosis, having only three life stages: egg, nymph, adult

I'm Special
— water striders can run along on top of the water's surface because of something called "surface tension". Where water meets air, a sort of barrier is set up, allowing objects heavier than water to stay up as long as the barrier is not broken. Water striders have their claws part way up their legs, instead of on their feet, so that the claws don't break through the surface tension barrier.
— the long legs of the water strider also help to spread the insect's mass out over a larger area. This also helps stop the insect from sinking. It's like your wearing snowshoes to spread your mass more evenly across the snow, allowing you to walk on top of the snow, rather than sinking in.

P.S.
— many of the true bugs related to water striders live on land and most are plant feeders
— if you were an entomologist (a person who studies insects), the only insects you would call "bugs" are those that belong to the orders Hemiptera or Homoptera. Some people place these two orders together.
— you can usually tell a bug apart from a beetle if you look at its back. The wing tips of a bug cross over, but a beetle's wings meet in a straight line down its back, never crossing.

Words to Learn
entomologist, incomplete metamorphosis, nymph, surface tension

Cicada

Order: *Homoptera*
Related Insects: hoppers, whiteflies, aphids, scale insects

Look at Me
— large, blackish, fly-like insect
— 2 pairs of clear wings
— wide body and head

Find Me
— adults usually live in trees
— nymphs live underground near the base of trees on the tree roots
— although cicadas are not easily seen, their loud buzzing noises, especially on hot days, are easy to hear and identify

Let's Eat
— nymphs feed on the roots of plants
— they have piercing-sucking mouthparts

My Life Story
— cicadas, like their relatives, undergo incomplete metamorphosis, with only three life stages: egg, nymph, adult
— the female makes a slit in a twig on a tree and lays her eggs
— when the nymphs hatch out, they drop to the ground and burrow under
— depending on the species, the nymph will stay in its burrow from 1-5 years. Some however, remain there for 17 years!
— at the end of the nymph stage, the nymph climbs out of its burrow, crawls up on a tree trunk and moults to become an adult

I'm Special
— cicadas are the loudest of all insects
— the males "sing" to attract a mate by vibrating two drum-like membranes on their abdomens

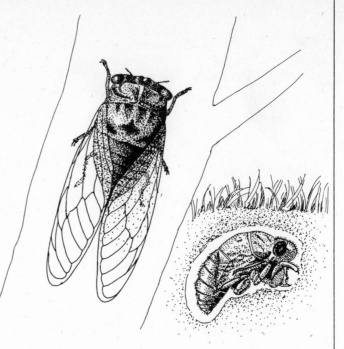

— cicadas are sometimes called hydro bugs because their buzzing-like noise sounds like the vibrations from heavy power lines

P.S.
— in Japan, some people keep cicadas in cages, like birds, so they can hear them sing
— the froghopper, a relative of the cicada, is well known because of the sudsy mass of "spit" produced on plant stems by its nymph

Words to Learn
abdomen, incomplete metamorphosis, membrane, moult, nymph